The Stress Owner's Manual

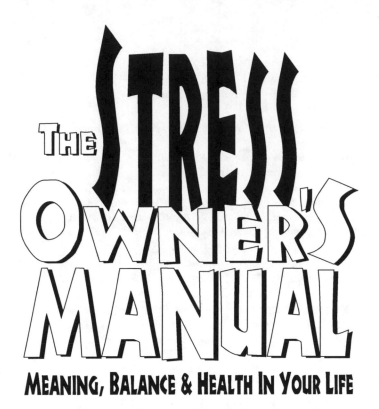

THE STRESS OWNER'S MANUAL

MEANING, BALANCE & HEALTH IN YOUR LIFE

ED BOENISCH, PH.D.

C. MICHELE HANEY, PH.D.

Impact 🕮 Publishers®, Inc.
ATASCADERO, CALIFORNIA 93423

Impact Publishers and colophon are registered trademarks of Impact Publishers, Inc.

Portions of this book were previously published under the title StressMap: Finding Your Pressure Points, © 1982, 1987, by C. Michele Haney and Edmond W. Boenisch, Jr.

ATTENTION ORGANIZATIONS AND CORPORATIONS:
This book is available at quantity discounts on bulk purchases for educational, business, or sales promotional use. For further information, please contact Impact Publishers, P.O. Box 6016, Atascadero, California 93406. Phone: 1-800-246-7228, e-mail: info@impactpublishers.com

Library of Congress Cataloging-in-Publication Data

Boenisch, Edmond W., 1947 —
    The stress owner's manual   :   meaning, balance & health in your life
  /   Ed Boenisch,   C. Michele Haney.
        p.   cm.
      Includes bibliographical references and index.
      ISBN 0-915166-84-4 (alk. paper)
        1.   Stress management.   I.   Haney, C. Michele, 1944 —
  II.   Title.
  RA785.B64   1996   96-26977
                                                                     CIP

Publisher's Note
This publication is designed to provide accurate and authoritative information in regard to the subject matter covered. It is sold with the understanding that the publisher is not engaged in rendering psychological, medical, or other professional services. If expert assistance or counseling is needed, the services of a competent professional should be sought.

Printed in the United States of America on acid-free paper
Map logos by Rob Sexton
Cover design by Sharon Schnare, San Luis Obispo, California
Published by **Impact 🗺 Publishers**®
POST OFFICE BOX 6016
ATASCADERO, CALIFORNIA 93423-6016
www.impactpublishers.com

Contents

Introduction

*S*tress management is all about finding *meaning, balance* and *health*.

Three statements by individuals living centuries apart sum up the key to effective stress management:

> *"Most folks are about as happy as they choose to be."*
> — Abraham Lincoln

> *"You can't teach a person anything, you can only help them find it within themselves."*
> — Galileo Galilei

> *"Most folks are about as stressed as they choose to be."*
> — Ed Boenisch and Michele Haney

If you really understand what these three quotes are saying, you understand what this book is all about. And you probably are doing quite a bit already to manage your stress levels.

Congratulations!

Even if these quotes make a lot of sense, we encourage you to read this book and renew your commitment to yourself, your health, your happiness, and ultimately to your longevity.

Because ultimately, effective stress management is all about...

The choices *you* make dozens of times each day about...
Living

"He who has a why to live for can bear with almost any how."
— Nietzche

Or Dying.

*"The mind is capable of holding a conversation with itself
that will end in death."*
— Russian Proverb

We invite you to read on
and choose today — and every day —
To Live!

What is This Thing Called Stress?

*I*f you are alive, you will experience stress. No one is immune. But even though stress comes with the territory, it comes without an owner's manual — until now. This book is a practical point-by-point guide to understanding and dealing with the stress we owners of human minds and bodies experience every day.

Touching a hot element on a stove or hearing a good joke both cause reactions. Each actually produces a type of stress. *Stress happens whenever your mind and your body react to some real or imagined situation.* Situations which cause stress reactions are called *stressors*.

Some stress is beneficial or desirable. Other types of stress, particularly if prolonged, can fatigue or damage your system to the point of malfunction or disease. Since *every* condition or event in your daily life causes some type or degree of stress, it is unrealistic and impossible for you to totally eliminate stress from your life! You actually *need* moderate levels of stress to help you stay alert and perform well. The only people totally free of stress are those who populate our cemeteries!

Dr. Hans Selye, the "father" of stress research, made the important distinction between stress which is harmful and that which is beneficial. Harmful stress can cause one to feel helpless, frustrated, disappointed. It can also cause physical as well as psychological damage. Selye called this *distress*. Other types of stress are beneficial and give a sense of achievement, satisfaction, fulfillment, meaning, balance, health. Such stress, which helps us to live longer and happier, he termed *eustress*.

It is not so much the stressor itself or the intensity of the stressor that makes stress beneficial or detrimental, but *your personal reaction* to the event or condition. A good example is flying: some people on the flight enjoy it tremendously and experience eustress, while others on the same flight become frightened or even hysterical and feel distress.

In Chapter 3, you'll meet two persons who experience the same stressors. One is successful in stress management and creates a lifestyle that is healthier, more balanced and more meaningful. The other tends to be distressed. As you read about them, keep asking yourself what makes them different.

You weren't born with undesirable reactions to stressors. You learned by watching others, by modeling from parents and teachers, by painful and pleasing experiences — how to react to different situations, and eventually develop habits that can persist. What kind of reactions to stressors have you learned? Ask yourself these two important questions:

1. What do *you* believe about your ability to deal with life, with stressors?

2. What kind of personal reaction to stressors are *you* willing to *choose*?

The answers to these two questions are the key to successful stress management.

The Universal, Instinctive, Primitive Stress Reaction

Being able to deal effectively with life, which is healthy, balanced stress management, must first begin with an understanding of how your mind and body react to life events, stressors. Remember the definition of stress: *Stress happens whenever your mind and your body react to some real or imagined situation.*

When you encounter a stressor, you respond both physically and psychologically. It all begins with a mental reaction that involves your beliefs about yourself and life. Your beliefs will determine how your body reacts and ultimately how well you will respond and possibly survive the constant stressors you experience in everyday living.

A *biological reaction* occurs that includes your muscles, gastro-intestinal system, brain, cardiovascular system, skin, and immune system. This reaction or activation of your body is caused by a radical and quick change in the normal chemical balance of your body.

Consider what you would think and feel if one night your sound sleep were disturbed by a strange sound you *think* you heard. You live alone. You are not sure if you heard anything. Sometimes the house does make strange noises on a cold and windy winter's night. Were you dreaming? Were there footsteps in the next room?

During those few agonizing moments when you still think you heard something, a stress response happens. It all begins with your *thought process* which triggers a chain reaction in your body. In this situation you would *not* experience any stress if you did not wake up.

But you *did* wake up, and you *think* there may be danger in the next room. Here's an extremely simplified look at what's going to go on in your mind and body:

You *believe* you are in danger and your brain (quickly, automatically and unconsciously) sends an electrical message that stimulates your pituitary gland, a very small gland located in the middle of your brain. The pituitary excretes a hormone, ACTH (AdrenoCorticoTropic Hormone) into your bloodstream. ACTH flows to the two glands located just above your kidneys, the adrenals, which increase their secretion of adrenaline and a series of other hormones, causing your body to become highly aroused, ready for action. The chemical change affects every cell in your body. This whole electrical and chemical process takes only about eight seconds!

During the same eight seconds, other electrical messages in the nerves cause changes in your heart, lungs, and muscles. Your whole body is quickly placed on alert, ready to react. Some of your muscles and blood vessels constrict, raising your blood pressure and supplying your major muscles with a rich supply of blood. Muscle tone increases dramatically, ready for quick and strong action. Remember the stories about men and women in highly stressful emergencies performing unbelievable physical feats, such as moving automobiles?

During the same eight seconds, your liver begins to quickly produce glucose which is a needed energy source for your brain and muscles. Your brain especially needs a more abundant supply of glucose-rich blood so it can increase its electrical activity and better control your body's actions. Your breathing rate quickens, which increases the oxygen supply in the blood so your muscles and brain can use the glucose more effectively. Your heart rate speeds up, increasing the amount of blood sent to different parts of your body. The parts that need more blood, your brain and muscles, are given top priority, while blood is diverted from other less critical organs such as your stomach and intestines. This basically interrupts your digestion, which is why under prolonged stress you may have digestive problems. Blood is also diverted from your hands and feet. Not only does this allow more blood to be used where it is needed (brain, large muscles, heart) but this action would also minimize excessive bleeding if your extremities were injured. A negative side effect: your hands and feet may become cold and clammy under stress.

Your senses become focused on the possible danger from something or someone in the next room. Your hearing becomes more acute. The pupils of your eyes dilate, increasing your vision sensitivity. The concentration of the clotting agent in your blood even increases. These last few body changes occur to help you prepare for a physical struggle. They are evolutionary remnants from your biological past, but in certain life or death situations these reactions are invaluable.

This whole process is a magnificently coordinated electrical and chemical alerting or your body for a possible "fight-or-flight" response. The process occurs quickly (remember, in about eight to ten seconds), unconsciously, and yet is a very normal response of your body to protect itself against possible harm. *How intense this reaction is, or how long it lasts, all depends on how stressful or threatening YOU perceive the situation to be.*

It is important for you to be able to recognize your unique physical symptoms of distress. Some of the more common ones are listed below.

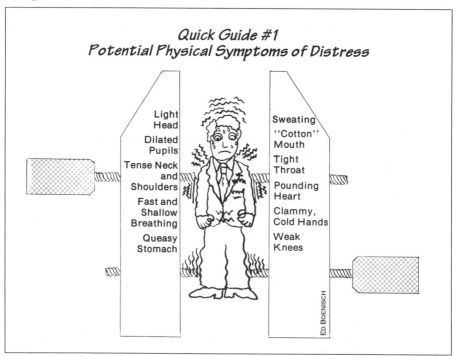

Quick Guide #1
Potential Physical Symptoms of Distress

Light Head
Dilated Pupils
Tense Neck and Shoulders
Fast and Shallow Breathing
Queasy Stomach

Sweating
"Cotton" Mouth
Tight Throat
Pounding Heart
Clammy, Cold Hands
Weak Knees

ED BOENISCH

Stress also involves *psychological reactions*. Since you are both a body and mind, stressors cause you to react psychologically. Some of the more common psychological indicators of a stress reaction are depicted on the next page.

Quick Guide #2
Potential Psychological Symptoms of Distress

In addition to understanding how you react physically to stressors, it is also important to know how your emotions respond under stress. Check each item which applies.

___apathy   ___high-pitched nervous laughter
___repression   ___dissatisfactions
___withdrawal   ___irritability
___forgetfulness   ___poor concentration
___anxiety   ___accident-proneness
___emotional tension or   ___overpowering urge to cry,
   alertness (being   run or hide
   "keyed up" or "hyper")   ___tendency to be easily startled
___nightmares

Knowing your own mental and physical symptoms will provide an early warning for you.

The Mind-Body Connection: A Matter of Life and Death

As we were describing your body's reaction to stress, we referred several times to what you were *thinking* and how your *mind* was responding. Remember again the definition of stress: Stress happens whenever *your mind and your body* react to some *real or imagined* situation.

Stress management has more to do with your mind (what you are perceiving, thinking and believing) than your body (how you are physically reacting). Your body's stress response begins with your brain, your mind. So the key to successful and effective stress management must also begin with what you are thinking and believing — how you perceive everything that happens to you. Doesn't it make sense to start with where your stress begins?

Scientists have begun to study the phenomenon of how thoughts, beliefs, or perceptions can affect the body's health, the connections between mind and body. It is called **PNI** or **P**sycho**N**euro**I**mmunology. There is evidence that the mind is not only capable, but regularly adjusts the biochemistry of the body.

Research in the last decade has discovered physical lines of communication between the brain and the immune system. Nerves connect the brain with organs such as the thymus and the spleen that in turn influence the immune system. Especially significant are the nerve connections between these organs and the limbic system of the brain that control emotions and the immune system.

This should be more than just interesting to you. There is literally a life and death implication for you! Your mind (*psycho*), through your nervous system (*neuro*), has the capability of affecting your immune system (*immunology*) which determines the existence and course of disease in your body. In other words, to a very large degree, *you can think yourself sick or well.* When your brain says, "I feel tired today," or "I can't seem to cope with anything," or "I'll probably come down with this crud everyone has," your immune system may respond by becoming tired and unable to fight off the crud.

Distress can effect the immune system. In a normal state your immune system seeks out and destroys harmful viruses and bacteria. When you experience excessive distress, the chemical changes in your body can alter the healthy functioning of your immune system. A weakened immune system can result in a susceptibility to the viruses and bacteria around and in you. This could explain why you may contract the common cold, flu, or infections that you would normally resist in less stressful, or eustressful, living conditions.

Your brain and your immune system are linked in a closed-circuit type of loop through your nervous system. In its simplest form, having this loop means that what you think can ultimately influence your health.

Pessimism, helplessness, hopelessness, depression, and loneliness are all states of mind that can negatively influence your body through your immune system. So the most powerful stress management tool, or "antidote," to the ill effects of distress can be a healthy mind. Specifically, you can do a lot to enhance the positive, health-producing connections between your brain and your body by:

— *Cultivating an optimistic or positive outlook* in your life by seeing the potentials in your life situations (believing and feeling that you have some control). See Quick Guide #3 on the next page.

— *Including humor in your life* since studies show a strengthened immune system for those who do take themselves less seriously (yet still take their life work very seriously). See Chapter 16, Mind Stress Buffers for more on humor.

— *Creating and maintaining strong social ties* and then being around people who love you for who you are. See Chapter 12, People Stress Buffers.

Quick Guide #3
Barriers to Personal Power and Change

Your mind can quickly strip you of much of your ability to believe in yourself and effectively cope with stressful situations. Your thoughts, beliefs, self-statements, and attitudes can empower you, or can be excuses for not taking action. Honestly assess how often you hear yourself say or think the following statements:

	ALWAYS			NEVER	
1. I've never done it before	1	2	3	4	5
2. It's too complicated	1	2	3	4	5
3. I don't have the time	1	2	3	4	5
4. It will never work for me	1	2	3	4	5
5. I've already tried that	1	2	3	4	5
6. It's a waste of time	1	2	3	4	5
7. I don't know how to...	1	2	3	4	5
8. It's really not that serious	1	2	3	4	5
9. I'm doing okay the way I am	1	2	3	4	5
10. I don't have the money	1	2	3	4	5
11. No one cares about what happens to me	1	2	3	4	5
12. I can't ...	1	2	3	4	5
13. I won't...	1	2	3	4	5
14. I'm afraid of what people will say	1	2	3	4	5
15. If it wasn't for (insert name here) I wouldn't have this problem	1	2	3	4	5
16. My life is too overwhelming right now; I can't add to it now by trying to change	1	2	3	4	5
17. It's too hard when the weather is (hot, icy, windy, nice)	1	2	3	4	5
18. My (job, education, family, etc.) is more important	1	2	3	4	5

How did you do? If your score is 54 or higher, you are probably in tune with how your mind, your attitudes, and your beliefs about yourself can empower you to cope effectively with whatever happens to you in life.

Too much strain can weaken your body's immune system and open it up to the potential for a host of stress-induced diseases. The science of psychoneuroimmunology is linking these conditions to how you think, what your mind perceives. It is important to note that not every instance of disease listed in *Quick Guide #4* is caused by stress or your mental condition. Research also teaches that your environment and genetic predispositions can influence your health. But there seems to be a growing body of research that indicates that excessive stress — distress — can make you more vulnerable to these diseases or illnesses.

You do have control of your mind and body and their reactions to stressors. Have you really accepted this reality?

Quick Guide #4
Potential Distress-Related Conditions

Place a check by any of the following illnesses/diseases that you have had in the last 12 months.

___ulcers	___insomnia or sleep disturbances
___heart attacks	___frequent urination
___strokes	___loss of appetite
___cancer	___excessive appetite
___hypertension (high blood pressure)	___rashes
	___diabetes
___headaches (tension and migraine)	___chronic fatigue
	___infections
___colitis	___allergies
___spastic colon	___asthma
___gastritis	___fainting spells
___chronic diarrhea or constipation	___stuttering and other speech difficulties
___queasiness (nausea)	
___excessive perspiration	___persistent or severe backache
___arthritis	___colds, flu, viral and bacterial infections
___muscle aches and tension	

If you have not done so already, consult your physician if you have any of these conditions, except perhaps a common cold. Is there a link between your distressful lifestyle and any of these illnesses?

A standard stress response is automatically called into action every time your mind perceives something as threatening. And when the belief is present that something is stressful, threatening, or dangerous the physical, all-or-nothing, flight-or-flight response takes place in your body. A physical stress response would occur if you were in an automobile accident and a very similar stress response (though perhaps less intense) will probably recur each time you relive the experience in your memory.

Stress and stress management are linked to a very basic yet important fact:

Your mind will react in the same way to what is real and what it imagines. To put it another way, your perception of reality is just as important as the reality itself.

For example, if you *believe* you are in danger or if you *think* you will be hurt, your mind kicks into action and prepares for the worst. It believes totally (perceives) that there is danger and it gears up to protect itself. In our earlier example — sounds in the night — you experience a stress reaction when you wake up and believe someone is in the next room. Your mind does not know what is happening in the next room. But, since it believes (perceives) there is danger, it prepares for danger by creating a physical and psychological response. Your mind's perception of reality is just as important as the reality itself.

This normally healthy and protective stress response can get in the way and be harmful in two ways:

1. If it happens too often when you *actually are* in some type of threatening situation, or

2. If it happens too often because *your mind only thinks you are* in a threatening situation.

In both instances, the full-blown physical and psychological stress response will happen which can create a big strain on your immune system which in turn can set you up for other problems, diseases, or illnesses like the ones in *Quick Guide #4.*

We are suggesting that you can have more control over your physical and psychological stress responses than you may realize.

In Chapters 2 and 3, we'll spend more time discussing the power of the mind. It is, after all, your mind which is the key to effective stress management and to your search for more meaning, balance and health in every part of your life.

2

How Do You Explain It?

"DON'T SPILL THE MILK!"

Every time Julie sat down at the dining room table, her young mind of thirty-two months heard the same thing from the others at the table. If it wasn't her mom, it was one of the other three brothers and sisters or dad who said, "Don't spill the milk!", "Be careful!", "You're always making a mess!", "You're so clumsy!" or something just as demeaning. And it seemed Julie was spilling more milk now than when she was younger. Everybody was more disappointed, frustrated and angry.

What had gotten into Julie?

"SIX MONTHS TO LIVE"

Cammie was in a state of shock after the doctor finished talking to her. Cammie's reaction was one of anger, denial and then resignation. The oncologist said the cancer would spread fast and that she would only have six months at most. Cammie took advantage of the short time she had and attended to all her affairs. She spent time with her children and family and friends.

After the funeral, her best friend observed that her death happened exactly six months after that fateful visit to the doctor.

Was this only a coincidence?

"DO I HAVE TO TAKE MATH?"

Over the past twenty years, thousands of eager, motivated individuals have talked to us, the authors, about taking college classes at the community colleges where we work. We have shared the excitement of their vision and answered their questions about the steps needed to start their first semester in college. We explained how to complete the various forms and talked about their dreams, all the while encouraging them in this new endeavor.

Then, one of the most common questions is asked: "What do I need to do to get a college degree?" With great care and sensitivity we calmly but eagerly talk about the various requirements: American Government, English, Humanities, Social Sciences, Fine Arts, courses in their major. But, then the prospective student mentions the four-letter word. "What about *math*?" Despite our encouragement and explanations about free tutoring and courses designed to build math skills, which every student already has from everyday experience, many say the same thing:

"But, I have never been any good at math."

"I always freeze up when I have to take a math test."

"I'll probably fail math."

"I'll never get a degree if I have to take all that math."

And despite our best efforts, some individuals don't even register. Others don't pass math. Still others never get the degree because of the math.

Why does this happen when they really do have the aptitude for math?

"BUT HE WAS SO HEALTHY"

They were so supportive of each other during those hard years while they successfully raised a large family. Even though they hardly knew each other on their wedding day because their marriage was arranged in the "old country," the marriage had lasted for fifty-six years. Anyone who knew them quickly felt how close they were. They were partners; they were soulmates.

Annie died quickly and unexpectedly of a stroke. Jake was overwhelmed with grief. He was in a state of shock and disbelief. He wandered around the house weeks after the funeral, crying and longing for Annie. His children and grandchildren spent time with him and took him into their homes. They truly loved him and showed it in so many ways. Jake truly appreciated their concern, but he missed Annie too much. Thirty-eight days after Annie's death, Jake joined her. He died peacefully in his sleep.

How could this happen when he was so healthy?

"WHY DO SOME SURVIVE?"

During both the Korean War and the Viet Nam Conflict, hundreds of our young men were captured and held as prisoners-of-war. The living conditions were primitive and their treatment at the hands of their captors was dehumanizing. Torture and beatings took place almost daily. Food was barely sufficient to maintain life. Communication with the other prisoners was forbidden. The questioning and psychological torture was relentless.

Some of our young men, who were very strong and healthy when they were captured, succumbed to illness and died within a relatively short time. Others, just as healthy upon capture, also experienced the same treatment in the same camps, yet lived for years and were repatriated.

Why the difference?

"HE HAD 'THE CURE' FOR CANCER"

In their book, *Getting Well Again*, Carl Simonton, Stephanie Matthews-Simonton, and James Creighton (pp. 22-23), relate a fascinating case. In the 1950's a man with lymphosarcoma, a malignancy of the lymph system, discovered that his physician was experimenting with a new wonder drug, Krebiozen, which was thought to be a possible cure for cancer. When the patient was given the drug, his condition improved dramatically. The symptoms of the disease — swollen glands, chest fluid, pain — disappeared after several weeks and he became ambulatory.

During his recovery, reports on the doubtful value of the new drug began to appear in the news. The patient's cancer began to reappear and his physical condition deteriorated quickly. The doctor told his patient that a refined, double-strength form of the drug had been developed. After several injections the patient's recovery was even more dramatic than before. Actually, the doctor had only injected sterile water, but the man remained symptom-free for several months.

Unfortunately, newspaper stories appeared with headlines which indicated that Krebiozen was a worthless drug for the treatment of cancer. Within a few days, the patient was *dead!*

How could this happen when he was recovering so well?

What Is the Real "Secret" to Meaning, Balance and Health?

Every one of these human tragedies has one element in common. It is the one element which is also the ultimate secret to successful stress management, and to finding more meaning, balance and health. The concept is so simple most people dismiss it and continue to spend lots of money and time in search of the "real" magical cure. They hear the secret and never recognize it or accept it for its simple power.

"The secret" has been known for centuries, said in different ways, always presenting the same concept and usually phrased in one sentence:

*"Our life is
what our thoughts make it."*
— Marcus Aurelius

*"He who has a why to live
can bear with almost any how."*
— Nietzsche

*"Most folks are about as happy
as they choose to be."*
— Abraham Lincoln

*"We are not what we think we are;
but, what we think, we are."*
— Norman Vincent Peale

*"Garbage in,
garbage out."*
— Computer maxim

*"The mind is capable of holding a conversation with itself
that will end in death."*
— Russian Proverb

*"You can't teach a person anything,
you can only help them find it
within themselves."*
— Galileo Galilei

*"Most folks are about as stressed
as they choose to be."*
— Ed Boenisch and Michele Haney

Your beliefs, positive attitude, your sense of control, what you think, your mindtalk, hope — it's all the same internal, human capacity which creates your destiny, for good or bad. You choose your future, your health, your living and, yes, even your dying, by what you think.

Your mind, your brain, and what it thinks is...

the key to a *healthier* body,
the key to more *balance* in your life,
the key to more *meaning and happiness*, and
the key to more *effective stress management*.

Can it be as simple as that?

Your brain, through what you think, literally controls your destiny. Do you *think* about the glass as half full or half empty? Do you *believe* you can have a successful, meaningful relationship? Do you have *faith* in your ability to climb 14,000-foot Long's Peak in Colorado? Do you have *hope* in your future as a bronze sculptor?

Are you willing to look closely at what's going on in your life by looking closely at what's going on inside your head?

Quick Guide #5
The Power of Your Mind

Rate yourself on how much you agree with
each of the following statements:

	ALWAYS				NEVER
1. I see life as challenging but exciting	5	4	3	2	1
2. Change is positive for me; it leads me to greater personal growth	5	4	3	2	1
3. I concentrate on what I can change and then do it	5	4	3	2	1
4. I know I can influence the events taking place around me	5	4	3	2	1
5. I think about how I can turn situations to my advantage	5	4	3	2	1
6. Even though situations are tough, I know I can usually find some way of feeling in control	5	4	3	2	1
7. I believe I am in control of my life	5	4	3	2	1
8. I accept that I am responsible for how I feel and what happens to me	5	4	3	2	1
9. I am hopeful about what lies in my future	5	4	3	2	1
10. I am aware of how much my mindtalk can make or break me	5	4	3	2	1

How did you do? The higher your score is above 30, the more you are in tune with the power of a positive attitude. Read on...

There are no "good" or "bad" situations in your life. The stress in your world is neutral. The dozens of events you experience every day are just that, events. They happen to you just like they happen to others. It's your reaction to every event which makes it "good" (eustress) or "bad" (distress).

Yes, it's true. There are "bad" things that happen to good people. Unfortunate accidents do take place. But, when you think about it, it does no good to become resentful and hold your anger and blame for even short periods of time. Your adult temper tantrums will not change the past or the present. But holding ill will can do a lot to make your todays and tomorrows more miserable than they have to be.

When you look at the dozens of events in each of your days, you can only point the finger at yourself and begin to accept the simple reality that *you* decide whether each situation is a burden or a blessing. *You* create your own distress by how *you choose* to interpret or view the events in your life. You cannot blame anyone or anything in your life for what is happening to you. You can't be angry and resentful toward your boss, significant other, children, God, friends, co-workers, pet, the government, or anything or anyone else.

To put it another way...

Living in your world with more meaning, balance and health involves:
> ten percent what happens to you, and
> ninety percent how you think about and then how *you react* to what happens to you.

Or, to put it still another way...

More successfully managing your stress and finding more meaning, balance and health is:
> ten percent action (learning and using stress management techniques), and
> ninety percent attitude (how and what you think).

These are the two A's of effective stress management:

> A...for the *Actions* you can learn which will help you to deal more effectively with distressful situations, and
> A...for the *Attitudes* you create and maintain in your mind.

It really is as simple as that!

The rest of *The Stress Owner's Manual* will help you:
1. Identify where your distress is located in each of six areas of your life (Chapters 4-9),
2. Design a prioritized plan to start managing your distress more effectively (Chapters 10-11),
3. Identify ways to develop a more positive, hopeful *attitude* (Chapter 3 mainly, but many sections of Chapters 12-22),
4. Learn important stress buffers and stress relief techniques *(actions)* (Chapters 12-22).

3

Preventive Maintenance: Making Up Your Mind

*W*e hope this chapter will be a personal wake-up call for you.

Since you're reading this book, you are probably looking for some ways to improve how you live your life and how you feel about it. Looking for more meaning, balance and health is admirable...

if you are willing to do something more
than just read a book
that is quickly placed on the shelf
or make a New-Year's-Eve type of resolution
that is quickly forgotten.

This book — and especially this chapter — is your personal invitation to:
- stop blaming everyone else for your problems,
- stop complaining, whining, and making excuses,
- stop avoiding reality,
- stop acting and believing as if you are the only one with the answers, and
- start taking responsibility for your own life by starting to take control of your mind.

During World War II, a German-Jewish psychiatrist, Viktor Frankl, coped with years of unspeakable horror in Nazi death camps. From his personal experiences he realized that the force that keeps us going day-by-day, year-by-year, in all types of life events, is our desire to find meaning in all we experience. Living means that events will happen because life is a series of events. Some events may bring suffering while others may bring joy. The ability to survive and find meaning in one's life is linked to our ability to find meaning in each event of our life, especially to find meaning in the suffering. After his release, he wrote in *Man's Search for Meaning*.

> *"If there is a purpose in life at all, there must be a purpose in suffering and dying. But no man can tell another what his purpose is. Each must find out for himself, and must accept the responsibility that his answer prescribes. If he succeeds he will continue to grow in spite of all indignities."*

Frankl is fond of quoting Nietzsche, "He who has a why to live can bear with almost any how."

> *"In the concentration camp every circumstance conspires to make the prisoner lose his hold. All the familiar goals in life are snatched away. What alone remains is 'the last of human freedoms' —the ability 'to choose one's attitude in any given set of circumstances, to choose one's own way.'"* (Preface, pp. 11-12).

Dr. Frankl made daily choices in the death camps when most would not even recognize the existence of any choices. Your challenge is to take back control of your mind and what you think. Your choice is to make up your mind to look at your life in a way that will bring you more meaning, balance and health.

If you are not convinced that your attitudes and beliefs are a big key to more meaning, balance and health, please go back and read Chapter 2 again, especially the six examples of people who gave up their lives because of what they believed. They had a choice and they chose against themselves.

So...how do you go about strengthening your beliefs or attitudes so that you can be as prepared as possible for what life will bring you?

We have found that there are four steps you can take.

1. THINK REAL

"Think real" is another way of saying: "Stop kidding yourself." Your mind is working constantly, evaluating everything you experience. Your thoughts, which will color your emotions and your day, may have a tendency to be negative and catastrophic. You can see it in the example of D.I. Stress (see sidebar).

To "think real" means you will want to practice monitoring your thinking so that you don't get into a mental rut. You can do this by spending a few minutes, some time each day, writing in a journal. List those events you want to forget but can't. Remember your thoughts about each event, about yourself, and about others. Challenge your mind by holding up a mirror of truth and reality to everything you were thinking. Are those things really true or false? Or are they "don't knows"? Remember, you have no way of knowing what the future is going to be and you have no way of knowing what someone else is thinking or will do unless you ask.

It will also be helpful to watch for thinking or even speaking that includes words such as *never, should, must, can't, always, ought.* These are big "hooks" that can drag you and others into conflict.

Thinking real also means you will want to seriously consider giving up on the belief that *you* know how people ought to act or how things ought to be. It is an easy trap to fall into. The media freely says what the Congress should do to solve our problems. The Congress freely says what the President should do or not do to make our world better. Deep down, you really do know how others should act or how they ought to be. You probably even do it to yourself, expecting yourself to get it right, to be perfect, every time. If you think about it, you are falling into the human trap of believing that the world would be a better (perfect?) place if everyone would just listen to you. You are like most people who would like to have it your way, all the time. Unfortunately, the job of being Master of the Universe is already taken and you don't have it. Watch what expectations you have about not only others, but yourself. Get real and think real about what you can and cannot do.

"Ever Have One Of Those Days?"

Let's look at two cousins, D.I. Stress and E.U.Stress, and the life events they experienced on Tuesday, the 30th of February. Coincidentally, their respective alarm clocks had failed, and each was an hour late. Here is how the day went. Notice how each responds to the same events (stressors). Each has a choice and each approaches the life events with an attitude — and D.I.Stress really has an attitude!

Stressors	D. I. Stress	E. U. Stress
Alarm did not go off. One hour late.	Angry, upset, worried. Rush to get ready. Make mistakes and lose more time. "This always happens to me. I will probably get fired."	Start to get upset but realize extra sleep felt refreshing. Use deep breathing exercises while dressing quickly. "I deserved the extra sleep. I made a mistake and I will cope with it. I'm not a failure because of it."
Carpool ride arrives.	Snap at friend, both lose temper. Breathing rate increases. Feel out of control. "This is going to be a horrible day. No one understands or supports me, ever."	Ask friend to call other rider and explain unfortunate delay. Grab oranges to share with friends in car. "This can happen to anyone. My friends will be there for me when I explain what happened."
Encounter heavy traffic. More time lost.	Become irritated at traffic. Cause everyone to get upset. "What a lousy day this is. No one knows how to drive anymore."	Discuss with others how you will adjust appointments. Talk slowly and confidently. Take time to compose self for rest of day. "I apologize if I have caused any inconvenience to you. I want you to know I am committed to being on time for myself and for you."

Meet first appointment 20 minutes late.	Try to rush through work. Make mistakes. Drop pen and bump head picking it up. Face becomes contorted and stays tense. Client becomes uneasy. "My day is going to be a disaster because it started off a disaster."	Apologize for inconvenience. Concentrate on relaxing muscles while listening closely to client. Have productive interview even though still behind schedule. "I want to be here for my client even if I am running behind."
Lunch hour delayed.	Eat quickly. Do not talk to anyone. Do not enjoy meal. Rush back to office with beginning of indigestion. "Even my lunch is a disaster. Today is just as bad as yesterday and tomorrow will be a disaster in some way, I just know it."	Call colleague before eating to inform him about 15-minute delay. Eat slowly, thinking about favorite hiking spot. Stop and wash face before going to meeting. "This is a refreshing break. I want to focus on the important tasks this afternoon."
Driving home in carpool.	Remember hassles of day. Tell fellow riders about all the problems. Stomach still upset. Shoulders and neck still stiff. Headache starting. All feel uneasy. "What a typical day — another tragedy I didn't deserve. Life is out to get me and my boss is a big part of it. She never under-stands me and is always picking on me."	Since not driving, take time to close eyes for a few minutes and relax muscles. Plan a peaceful evening as a way of being good to yourself for challenging day."Work's over and I am going to make this evening special. I made the best out of a bad beginning. There was no doubt I could do it."
Evening at home.	Gulp down a stiff drink. Feel angry about day. Rush through supper. Stomp around house. Kick dog. "I'll show them they can't treat me that way. I won't take the blame anymore."	Take a long, soaking bath. Fix favorite meal while listening to favorite music. Eat slowly. Spend time with pet. "It feels so comforting to relax after such a challenging day. Tomorrow will be a great one."
Bedtime.	Get angry again when setting alarm. Take 45 minutes to fall asleep. Muscles still tight. Toss and turn all night. "What a bummer. Life's not worth it if it keeps going like this. I can't ever win or get ahead."	Read a favorite novel in bed after spending a few minutes in journal mak-ing a gratitude list of the day's happenings. Drift off to sleep relaxed and calm. "There is so much I can be thankful for if I just look and keep everything in perspective."

2. ACCEPT RESPONSIBILITY

This step to a healthier more satisfying attitude is a real challenging one for many. Each moment of every day you can choose how you are going to be with each event and with each person. John Milton said it well:

> *"The mind is its own place,*
> *and in itself can make heaven out of Hell,*
> *a hell of Heaven."*

To accept responsibility means that you cannot slip into the easy trap of believing everything "bad" that happens to you is someone else's fault. Events are happening all the time —that's what time and life are all about. Sometimes you can play a more active role in what is happening; sometimes you are not much of a player. It really does no good to try to find someone or something to blame. If you don't like life events, if you tend to get angry or hurt and try to rebel against what you don't like — then your life will probably be more frustrating, less meaningful, less fulfilling and less healthy than it has to be. The choice really is yours to accept the responsibility for your own feelings and outlook on the events that happen in your life.

How do you learn to accept responsibility and to stop blaming? Go back to step one, Think Real, and use the same techniques. Challenging your thoughts and having them work *for* you is your key.

3. SEE POSSIBILITIES

Psychologists Gary McKay and Don Dinkmeyer, in their book, *How You Feel is Up to You,* invite their readers to imagine a delightful yet powerful scene: the eagle, flying over the Grand Canyon, sees it as a "...huge, deep crevice in the earth." Yet to an ant looking up from the canyon floor, it is "...composed of huge mountains, reaching to the sky" (page 24).

How do you view your life? Is it a series of mistakes and punishments because life is cruel and unforgiving and people are against you? Or do you see the possibilities, even in the events that look like failures?

We encourage you to see the possibilities, by first being aware of the strengths you possess and the accomplishments you have achieved. Use your journal to do a soul-searching, honest listing of everything you have going for yourself.

Next, remember every day those life events that you wish you could forget but can't. Look at them objectively and honestly. What's the simple truth about them? For E.U.Stress (sidebar), waking up an hour late did not mean that he was a total failure, as he might have had a tendency to think and believe. Rather, he thought and really believed: "I made a mistake and I will cope with it. I'm not a failure because of it. I deserved the extra sleep."

You can also help yourself see the possibilities by dreaming realistically about what you want to accomplish each day, each year, and the rest of your life. Write your dreams down in that journal we keep mentioning and hoping you will acquire for yourself. Share them with important others in your life. Review them frequently.

4. GO FOR IT

We have two suggestions for this last step in training your mind to be your best friend rather than your downfall. First, while it is beneficial to think about what you want to be and how you are going to get there, it is more important to take your goals and start making them a reality. Check out the six goal-setting criteria on the next two pages.

Second, you will be more successful "going for it" if you are respectful of others' rights while honoring your own. In other words, be assertive in your life. Chapter 12 has more thoughts on this suggestion. At the same time enrich your life by taking risks, maybe small safer ones at first, and being more empathetic, compassionate and loving to others. History has many lessons about the ultimate success and power in love and cooperation rather than hate and dominance.

"These, then, are my last words to you:
Be not afraid of life.
Believe that life is worth living
and your belief will help you create that fact."
— William James, 1800's psychologist

Keep Your Eye on the Goal

Goal Setting: Your potential for success will increase dramatically if every goal you choose contains the following six elements:

1. Written

Improving your life in some way is a challenge. It helps to have both the desire to want to do something and the discipline to follow through with it. It is so easy to "forget" your good intentions. "Out of sight" really does become "out of mind." Keep your goals written and visible and thereby increase your potential for success.

2. Specific (measurable)

When you have a clear picture in your mind of what you want to accomplish, it is easier for you to write it down and then create it. Here are some examples:

Poor: "I have to take better care of myself."

(Notice the tone of urgency and drivenness with the "have to." But it is not specific.)

Better. "I want to lose weight."

Best: "I will lose 1 pound a week."

(This is specific and measurable. "I will" creates a sense of determination that can help create success.)

3. Realistic

Goals can be frustrating and demoralizing if they are unrealistic. Set yourself up for as much success as possible by writing goals that create a challenge yet are achievable.

Unrealistic and Unhealthy:

"I will lose 10 pounds before the class reunion next weekend."

More realistic:

"I will lose 1 pound every two weeks by starting this Saturday on a gradually more challenging walking program, combined with eliminating ALL my snacking between meals and before bedtime."

4. Target Date

Your chances for success are increased when you can "see" when your goal will be completed. A realistic target date will give you a clear focus with both a beginning and an ending.

Good: "I will lose 10 pounds in one year."

(This goal is specific, measurable and realistic. It even has a target date, one year; but it is probably too easy to forget about over a 12-month period.

Better: "I will lose 1 pound every two weeks for 20 weeks, starting this Saturday."

5. Shared and supported
You may need some professional advice before you start certain goals. You definitely should consider asking at least one other person to support you while you work on your goal. This person's role is to regularly ask you how you are doing with your goal and to encourage you, lovingly but firmly, if you falter.

6. Celebrate!
Each time you accomplish one of your goals, pause and do something to reward your successful efforts. Be good to yourself!

Here is the same goal stated in two different ways:
1. "I have to do something to take care of myself!" (Said to yourself in desperation.)

2. "I will discuss my goal with my physician during my Thursday appointment. If my doctor supports me, I will lose 1 pound every two weeks for 20 weeks.

Realistic, specific, measurable, ending date and some support.

"I will start this Saturday in two ways:
A. I will begin by briskly walking 1/4 mile every day in the park after work and increase my distance 1/4 mile every 5th day until I achieve three miles a day.

Beginning target date.

Realistic, specific and measurable.

"I will chart my walking progress each day and keep this written goal and progress chart on the refrigerator.

Written, measurable.

"B. Beginning today, I will eliminate all snacks between meals and before bedtime. I will chart my success each day. I will keep a good supply of no-fat, low-cal snacks.

Realistic, written, specific.

"I will give Todd a copy of this goal since he agreed to call me every Friday evening before 9 p.m. I will review my progress (charts) with him and tell him how motivated I am with this goal.

Support

"After every brisk walk, I will treat myself to a cold glass of my favorite fruit juice and a warm bath.

Celebrate!

"When I achieve my goal of losing 10 pounds, I will treat myself to a new pair of slacks and I will ask Todd to join me for a Sunday hike to our favorite spot."

Celebrate!

What is the Plan of The Stress Owner's Manual?

The next several chapters present a series of six questionnaires — "maps" — to help you identify the stressors in each area of your life. Here is a sampling of some of the items involved:

- •PEOPLE

  Family, friends, marriage, divorce, widowhood, activities, and giving and receiving of love.

- •MONEY

  Material goods and possessions, salary, savings, budgets, investments, retirement, bills, and credit.

- •WORK

  Life's central activity, means of livelihood, and the relationship to the people with whom you work and interact. This area applies to work in or out of the home as well as to schoolwork. Also included are meal preparations, errands, grocery shopping, house repairs, vehicle repairs, housecleaning, laundry, childcare, yardwork, and mending.

- •BODY

  Sports, exercise, relaxation, diet, hygiene, medical care, physical surroundings, and life spaces.

- •MIND

  Fulfillment, self-discipline, reading, meaningfulness, humor, mental relaxation, peace, joy, spirituality.

- •LEISURE

  Social life, hobbies, cultural activities, creative endeavors, community work, and volunteer organizations.

  Mapping the areas of your life that *lead* to stress reactions is not your final goal, of course. Once the stressors are found, you must decide which you are willing to change. We have provided suggestions for modifying your life to reduce your distress. As you progress through this material, you will quickly discover that you can have more control over stress and your reactions to it than you probably thought possible.

Even though you will examine each of the six areas of your life separately, you should always keep in mind that these areas are inseparable. Visualize them as working together to create a balanced, positive, *holistic* approach to health!

The six "StressMap" chapters (4-9) each include a brief introduction and a self-examination. This process of *stressor mapping* is the *first* step in a successful stress management program. The "maps" will help you identify the stressors in your life in six major areas: PEOPLE, MONEY, WORK, LEISURE, MIND, and BODY.

Don't be surprised if you discover that some areas of your life have more stress than others; that's what we hope you *will* learn. This process, involving the six stress maps, is very individual and personal. Even people who live or work closely together will not react to stressors in the same way.

The maps will be useful primarily as a way to *find* your stressors. The second step in stress management is to decide what you want to *do* about them. The Stress and Relief Buffers sections, Chapters 12-22, are designed to help you systematically and inexpensively learn lifelong skills for effective stress management.

Instructions for Following the Six StressMaps:

Answering: Respond to each statement the way you generally feel at this time in your life. Rate every statement by circling the number that corresponds to how you feel. The zero (0) column means "no" or that the statement "does not apply." Columns 1 to 5 indicate "yes," and show *how much* you are bothered or stressed by the situation. The higher the number you mark, the more stressed you feel.

Scoring: At the end of each map, add up the total for each column. For every circle in column 5 ("Bothers me a lot"), add 5 points to your score. For every circle in column 4, add 4 points, and so on. Any response in the zero (0) column receives no points. Enter your total score for each StressMap on the composite map on pages 54-55. Follow these same procedures for answering and scoring all six StressMaps in Chapters 4-9. P.S. Don't let these instructions stress you — it's really very simple!

4

People StressMap

Relationships arc a very important and yet very complex aspect of life. Are you single, with a partner, in a more traditional marriage, widowed, a single-parent, divorced, separated, childless? Relationships include our immediate and extended family, those we find in the workplace or school as well as acquaintances and associates.

Consider the endless activities and time involved in the management, cultivation and growth of relationships: meals, errands, vacations, cleaning, repairing, laundry, caring for children/parents/pets, telephoning, planning, social obligations...*hold it!* Work stress is a whole other topic! (We'll discuss that in Chapter 6.)

Whatever your situation with other people in your life, *balance* is the key. You are not alone if you find the activities of managing your relationships with others tipping the balance and consuming more time than you would like. An important key to achieving and maintaining balance is constantly working toward and then enjoying some or all of the following: expressing feelings, spending time together, enjoying the company of another, listening, sharing, giving, loving, committing, touching, recommitting, hugging, and recommitting, again.

Giving and receiving love are more important than all the "activities" and "duties" with which we tend to fill our days. Giving and receiving tip the balance back toward intimate relationships of mutual growth and fulfillment.

How are your relationships?

SYMPTOMS OF PEOPLE STRESS

Stress with people can make you feel:
- lonely
- irritated
- frustrated
- misunderstood
- overwhelmed
- exhausted by the responsibilities, leaving little energy for the loving.

Do you allow the daily activities and duties to create a burden of pressure on you? The set of statements you will now consider is a start in choosing and creating a balance in your relationships.

People StressMap

	DOES NOT APPLY (NO) 0	BOTHERS ME A LITTLE 1	2	3	4	BOTHERS ME A LOT 5

1. The children are growing up and leaving home.   0   1   2   3   4   5

2. I recently became separated and/or divorced.   0   1   2   3   4   5

3. Our family needs to spend more time together.   0   1   2   3   4   5

4. I feel at a loss in dealing with children.   0   1   2   3   4   5

5. I have recently had an addition to the family (birth, adoption).   0   1   2   3   4   5

6. I have trouble getting along with my relatives and/or friends.   0   1   2   3   4   5

7. I wish I had a family (partner, spouse, children).   0   1   2   3   4   5

8. Someone close has recently died.   0   1   2   3   4   5

9. I am facing the problems associated with elderly parents/relatives.   0   1   2   3   4   5

10. Too much of my time is spent doing things for others.   0   1   2   3   4   5

11. My relationship with my spouse/partner could be better.   0   1   2   3   4   5

12. I have difficulty forming close relationships with (underline all that apply) friends, co-workers, relatives, children, spouse, partner, in-laws.   0   1   2   3   4   5

13. I wish I enjoyed sexual experiences more.   0   1   2   3   4   5

14. When I am upset with someone close, I have difficulty expressing my feelings, either positive or negative.   0   1   2   3   4   5

15. I am a widow/widower.   0   1   2   3   4   5

16. There is a lack of intimacy in my life.   0   1   2   3   4   5

17. I am a stepparent.   0   1   2   3   4   5

18. I have trouble saying "no" to anyone who asks me for something.   0   1   2   3   4   5

19. I find it difficult to ask for help.   0   1   2   3   4   5

20. I am a single parent.   0   1   2   3   4   5

21. I find it difficult to accept constructive criticism without reacting defensively.   0   1   2   3   4   5

Total your score for people stress (you may find it helpful to refer to the instructions for scoring on page 29).

Total Score:_____

If your score is:

21 or less: You are probably dealing effectively with the pressures of people. Congratulations!

22 to 33:   This is an area you should examine more closely. Your stress level is high enough that you could in the near future experience some physical or mental signs of distress.

over 33:   People stress is signaling danger ahead! Please take time now to heed the warning and turn to Chapter 12. There you can reduce your speed and examine the Stress Buffers designed for immediate implementation in the area of people stress. Exceeding this level should be a serious warning to you. Don't delay in taking action!

5

Money StressMap

*H*ow do you view money? Is it a burden or a source of joy? Do you manage it or does it drive you? One secret to minimizing stress in this area is to accept the almost inevitable fact that the quality of your life depends on having some of it and managing it well. All the other areas of your life — people, mind, leisure, body, and work — are affected by the presence or absence of money. Material goods and possessions, your career, salary, investments, savings, bills, credit, income tax, the lottery, and your budget are all associated with the financial area.

How do you view money? What do you believe about it? Is it a source of happiness or the root of evil? Are finances a topic that will almost inevitably create friction? Is money a means to an end or the end itself?

SYMPTOMS OF MONEY STRESS

Financial stress can make you feel:
- helpless
- frustrated
- angry

It is a major source of marital conflict. But it is possible for money and finances to be a source of happiness (eustress). This next set of questions is a first step to help you keep the financial aspect of your life in perspective.

Money StressMap

	DOES NOT APPLY (NO)	BOTHERS ME A LITTLE				BOTHERS ME A LOT
	0	1	2	3	4	5

1. I recently received a cut in my salary/wages/contract.   0   1   2   3   4   5

2. There is a large mortgage on my home/condo.   0   1   2   3   4   5

3. I find myself trying to "keep up with the Joneses."   0   1   2   3   4   5

4. I worry about being able to provide my children with the things they need/want, especially a college education.   0   1   2   3   4   5

5. I or my partner lost a job recently.   0   1   2   3   4   5

6. I have many bills to pay.   0   1   2   3   4   5

7. I have charged too much on my credit cards.   0   1   2   3   4   5

8. I feel financially insecure.   0   1   2   3   4   5

9. I have difficulty managing a budget.   0   1   2   3   4   5

10. My income is failing more and more to keep up with expenses.   0   1   2   3   4   5

11. I have been delaying a savings or investment program.   0   1   2   3   4   5

12. I seem to have lots of financial concerns: higher taxes, lots of repairs, care for aging parents, higher costs for everything.   0   1   2   3   4   5

Total your score for money stress (you may find it helpful to refer to the instructions for scoring on page 29).

Total Score:_____

If your score is:

12 or less: You are probably dealing effectively with the pressures of money. Congratulations

13 to 36:   This is an area you should examine more closely. Your stress level is high enough that you could in the near future experience some physical or mental signs of distress.

over 36:   Money stress is signaling danger ahead! Please take time now to heed the warning and turn to Chapter 13. There you can reduce your speed and examine the Stress Buffers designed for immediate implementation in the area of money stress. Exceeding this level should bea serious warning to you. Don't delay in taking action!

6

Work StressMap

*W*ork stress touches almost everyone: the rodeo cowboy, the nurse, the President of the United States. You do not have to be receiving a salary or working full time to experience it. If you are a student, work part-time, or have a career in the home, distress is a possibility.

The "average" worker spends eight hours a day, five days a week, fifty weeks a year on the job. This is an investment (or loss, depending on how you look at it!), of approximately 2,000 hours every year. Since a career can be so time-consuming, it may be impossible for some to separate the career from the rest of living. The job literally becomes life, twelve hours a day, evenings and weekends for some who *believe* it will be this way.

How stressful is it for you to deal with work tasks day after day? Do you have deadlines? Do you believe you have to be competent and successful all the time? How do you react to all those problems that do not have an immediate solution? What are your reactions to the stressors in your job? Some may feel frustrated, angry, or overwhelmed. Others may try to escape by believing they can't take it and then unconsciously getting sick. Others still may disengage their overwhelming feelings by doing busy work that has no relation to the job, or by socializing away the hours. Are you the type who fights off the pressures and demands by pushing even harder, working faster, or longer? Has work ever been an activity that adds to your general fulfillment and happiness?

Since a means of livelihood can be so different for everyone and can consume so much of each day, you should spend some *extra* time on the following questionnaire, making each item as personal as possible. This questionnaire is also for students, homemakers, non-traditional job-holders, anyone who works inside or outside the home! Substitute appropriate words and phrases to fit your situation.

You may find it hard to accept that your job is a major cause of stress. Or you may believe that you have no power to change your situation, so why get into it? You may feel you would be more stressed if you were to admit that so much of your time is spent at an activity that is making life progressively more difficult the longer you stay in it. You may believe you are trapped in a no-win situation; but change is an option. Maybe it is a change of careers. Or maybe a change in all those other factors that can make a job less stressful. Or maybe it is a quick trip to the unemployment lines in your area to see and feel what it would be like to not have a job. Or maybe it is a change in attitude and a revitalization of the powerful and positive feelings and beliefs you had the first few days on the job. Remember?

SYMPTOMS OF WORK STRESS:

- irritated
- overwhelmed
- pressured
- dissatisfied

React to the following list as it relates to your situation. Then be innovative and flexible in your solutions.

Work StressMap

	DOES NOT APPLY (NO)	BOTHERS ME A LITTLE				BOTHERS ME A LOT
	0	1	2	3	4	5

1. Deadlines are a daily part of my job.   0 1 2 3 4 5

2. I have a problem completing work assignments because of the many interruptions.   0 1 2 3 4 5

3. After leaving the job, I generally complete work I have not had time for during the day.   0 1 2 3 4 5

4. I find it difficult to work with some of my co-workers.   0 1 2 3 4 5

5. I need to take some college courses or upgrade training in order to keep or advance in my job.   0 1 2 3 4 5

6. I find it difficult to find meaning or satisfaction in my job.   0 1 2 3 4 5

7. I continue to take on new job responsibilities without letting go of others.   0 1 2 3 4 5

8. There is little variety or challenge in my job.   0 1 2 3 4 5

9. I often feel overwhelmed with the demands of my job.   0 1 2 3 4 5

10. When I am under pressure I tend to not respond positively.   0 1 2 3 4 5

11. I wish there were more harmony/cooperation among the people with whom I work.   0 1 2 3 4 5

12. My job is emotionally demanding.   0 1 2 3 4 5

13. I feel burnout and want to change jobs/careers but seem unable to take the first step.   0 1 2 3 4 5

14. I find it difficult to deal with issues that do not have immediate or clear solutions.   0 1 2 3 4 5

15. I find it difficult to relax during breaks/lunch even when I do take them.   0 1 2 3 4 5

16. On my way to and from work, I tend to rehash the problems of the day.   0 1 2 3 4 5

17. When starting work projects, I find it difficult to become immediately involved or stay focused.   0 1 2 3 4 5

18. My job is at home. I do not get weekends — or even evenings! — off.   0 1 2 3 4 5

19. When hit by questions from all sides, I cannot
    answer or make a decision.   0   1   2   3   4   5

20. I am overwhelmed with the responsibility of
    being a perfect employee, spouse/partner and/or
    parent at the same time.   0   1   2   3   4   5

21. I am concerned about the possibility of a merger/
    layoff/downsizing by my employer.   0   1   2   3   4   5

Total your score for word stress (you may find it helpful to refer to the
instructions for scoring on page 29).

                                    Total Score:_____

If your score is:

20 or less: You are probably dealing effectively with the pressures
                    of work. Congratulations!

21 to 60:   This is an area you should examine more closely. Your stress
                    level is high enough that you could in the near future experience
                    some physical or mental signs of distress.

over 60:   Work stress is signaling danger ahead! Please take time now to
                    heed the warning and turn to Chapter 14. There you can reduce
                    your speed and examine the Stress Buffers designed for
                    immediate implementation in the area of work stress. Exceeding
                    this level should be a serious warning to you. Don't delay in
                    taking action!

7

Leisure StressMap

"*When I get everything done on my list, I will give myself some leisure time.*"

"*Leisure is for the rich, who else can afford it?*"

People who have beliefs like this seem to see leisure as a means of reducing stress when it becomes unbearable or they see leisure as a luxury. But leisure should not be the last resort — the *reaction* to a stressful lifestyle. Ideally, leisure should be a richly diverse "shopping list" of activities used regularly to *prevent* life from becoming too stressful.

Do you know what specifically helps you mentally and physically to reduce the effects of stressors? Have you explored social events, hobbies, cultural activities, community involvements and organizational memberships as potential sources of leisure? Do you ever find yourself maintaining a leisure activity even when it becomes a distasteful burden? Which of your leisure activities are free, take only a few minutes of time yet produce a wealth of joy, satisfaction, peace of mind, relaxation or fulfillment?

After writing this section, I (Ed) realized how "uptight" I was about continuing to belong to a certain professional organization. When I decided (three minutes ago) that I would not renew my membership and would not "buy into" the beliefs that I should attend the functions, I was so relieved. At the same time, I realized how therapeutic and fulfilling bronze sculpting has become. I recommitted to continuing my regular sessions of sculpting in my special corner of the family room.

SYMPTOMS OF LEISURE STRESS

Stress in the leisure area may result in feelings of:
- guilt
- confusion
- some people may feel overwhelmed
- frustrated.

The map which follows can help you determine the effectiveness of leisure in your life.

Leisure StressMap

	DOES NOT APPLY (NO)	BOTHERS ME A LITTLE				BOTHERS ME A LOT
	0	1	2	3	4	5

1. I have very little time for hobbies or pastimes. 0 1 2 3 4 5

2. I would like to spend more time in leisurely pursuits that get me out of the house or apartment. 0 1 2 3 4 5

3. I wish I spent more time just relaxing by talking with my friends. 0 1 2 3 4 5

4. I have put off learning something I think would be fun and fulfilling. 0 1 2 3 4 5

5. I would like to contribute more of my time to community activities or volunteer projects. 0 1 2 3 4 5

6. I wish my leisure interests were more varied. 0 1 2 3 4 5

7. I would like to spend more time in quiet, private, leisurely activities. 0 1 2 3 4 5

8. I would like to participate more in relaxing social or club activities. 0 1 2 3 4 5

9. When I have a break in my schedule I have difficulty relaxing either mentally or physically. 0 1 2 3 4 5

10. Holidays, weekends or time off are not as relaxing or enjoyable as I would prefer. 0 1 2 3 4 5

Total your score for leisure stress (you may find it helpful to refer to the instructions for scoring on page 29).

Total Score: _____

If your score is:

10 or less: Probably dealing effectively with the pressures of leisure.

11 to 30: This is an area you should examine more closely. Your stress level is high enough that you could in the near future experience some physical or mental signs of distress.

over 30: Leisure stress is signaling danger ahead! Please take time now to heed the warning and turn to Chapter 15 Stress Buffers designed for immediate implementation in the area of leisure stress. Exceeding this level should be a serious warning to you. Don't delay in taking action.

8

Mind StressMap

Your ability to reason, imagine, calculate, and verbalize makes you unique. Your mind is a powerful tool, but are you controlling it or is it controlling you?

Norman Vincent Peale said:

"You are not what you think you are;
but, what you think, you are."

Your mind is capable of hoping and believing. And what you believe, you create in yourself and in your world. If you don't believe this, try this brief experiment. Imagine yourself walking into your kitchen and opening the refrigerator. Imagine taking out a lemon and cutting it in half. Then imagine taking half the juicy, cold lemon and taking a *big* bite. Any reaction? Most people have some extra salivation. If you did, your mind believed you were tasting a lemon and it created a reality — salivation. Our minds are powerful and can be our friends or enemies in our efforts with stress management and the creation of a meaningful, balanced, and healthy lifestyle.

Some individuals use their mental powers to memorize large amounts of information or even entire books. Others master several languages. Many receive multiple educational degrees for their knowledge in a number of disciplines. Some develop themselves by reading extensively. All these individuals are not much different from you. *The one trait that probably sets them apart is that they have learned that they can control their destinies by what they think.* These people have *thought of themselves and believed* in themselves as learned, successful, rich, lovable, or anything else — and their intellect, their thoughts, their beliefs, have created the action which led to that reality. *You* must take the blame for your own failures...and the credit for your successes. *Now is the time to stop blaming God, life, the government, your spouse/partner, children, co-workers, boss, the pets, for what is happening in your life*. Begin assessing how much you are actually creating your life through your mind and what it thinks.

The mind is also our link to the spirit. In times of distress or crisis, many individuals seek comfort and help in prayer of some sort. A belief in God, Buddha, Allah, a Life Force, a Supreme Being, or whatever is meaningful to you can be a powerful stress reduction technique, not to mention a profound source of peace and fulfillment. We humans all have a spiritual nature, whether or not we subscribe to a particular belief or faith. Has your spirituality been a resource in the past or pushed aside in the hustle and bustle of daily activities?

What are you doing, on a regular basis, to develop your unique mental and physical talents? Do you believe you are lovable? Are you self-confident?   Have you been involved with formal or informal education? Is reading, both professional/self-help and leisure, a regular part of your life? Have you taught yourself how to relax your mind? Can you concentrate? Do you remember and learn what you want? Do you share ideas with others and learn from the ensuing discussion? Are you a positive person? Do you monitor and challenge your beliefs so that they are used to help you achieve your goals?

SYMPTOMS OF MENTAL STRESS

Mind stress can lead to:
- confusion and powerlessness
- inability to make decisions
- anger
- loneliness
- fear
- apathy
- forgetfulness
- depression
- emotional tension and alertness (being "keyed up")
- nightmares
- dissatisfaction
- irritability
- poor concentration
- strong urge to cry, run or hide
- tendency to be easily startled

How about you? The following StressMap will help.

Mind StressMap

	DOES NOT APPLY (NO)	BOTHERS ME A LITTLE				BOTHERS ME A LOT
	0	1	2	3	4	5

1. I find it difficult to feel any fulfillment, joy, or peace in my life.   0 1 2 3 4 5

2. I would like to read self-help books.   0 1 2 3 4 5

3. I tend to blame others for any situations I don't like.   0 1 2 3 4 5

4. I know what is important in my life.   0 1 2 3 4 5

5. I wish I knew how to be more in control of my feelings.   0 1 2 3 4 5

6. I find it difficult to discipline myself so I can accomplish goals I really want.   0 1 2 3 4 5

7. I want to feel more enthusiastic and positive about life.   0 1 2 3 4 5

8. I wish I felt more worthwhile and important as a person.   0 1 2 3 4 5

9. I find it difficult to remember things.   0 1 2 3 4 5

10. I feel restless.   0 1 2 3 4 5

11. I would like my life to have more meaning and purpose.   0 1 2 3 4 5

12. I want more spirituality in my life.   0 1 2 3 4 5

13. I find it difficult to laugh at myself or see the humor in some situations like others do.   0 1 2 3 4 5

14. I would like to find and use ways to relax my mind.   0 1 2 3 4 5

15. I am not enjoying my life.   0 1 2 3 4 5

Total your score for mind stress (you may find it helpful to refer to the instructions for scoring on page 29).

Total Score:_____

If your score is:

15 or less: Probably dealing effectively with the pressures of mind stress.

16 to 45:   This is an area you should examine more closely. Your stress level is high enough that you could in the near future experience some physical or mental signs of distress.

over 45:   Mind stress is signaling danger ahead! Please take time now to heed the warning and turn to Chapter 16 Stress Buffers designed for immediate implementation in the area of mind stress. Exceeding this level should be a serious warning to you. Don't delay in taking action!

9

Body StressMap

"I *already push myself a lot; why should I push even more by playing racquetball?"*

"I run around all day trying to keep up with the children, I don't need to go jog!"

"I watch my diet; I'm not overweight...that much."

"Relax? Sure, I relax when I finally get to sleep."

Do you ever find yourself making some or all of these statements? Don't they sound like excuses, false beliefs? If you find yourself thinking or saying something like this, then you may be ignoring one of your most valuable, and *irreplaceable*, resources, your body and its health.

The connection is simple yet incredibly important: when your physical well-being is neglected or abused, your overall performance is threatened. If you experience physical stress, you may feel tired, sluggish or unmotivated. Some people start experiencing more illnesses; others resort to food, alcohol, cigarettes, aspirin, prescription tranquilizers or pain-killers, or more caffeine to reduce tension, or simply become edgy and irritable.

Do you believe that physical conditioning is a luxury? Do you say to yourself that you don't have time to think about sports, exercise, relaxation, diet, hygiene, medical care, and physical surroundings? Do you tell yourself that you can live without all the latest health "fads"? Have you ever considered how much you could be shortening your life by shortchanging your physical well-being?

SYMPTOMS OF BODY STRESS

There is a lot of research that indicates that a (dis)stressful lifestyle can contribute to or hasten the appearance of the following:

- tense neck and shoulders
- cold or clammy hands
- bruxism (grinding the teeth)
- headaches/migraines
- light headedness
- queasy stomach
- excessive perspiration
- "cotton mouth"
- pounding heart
- weak knees
- anxious, nervous, jittery, jumpy feelings
- loss of appetite or excessive appetite
- loss of energy, fatigue
- nervous habits: nail biting, neck rubbing, foot or finger tapping

(Note: If someone has any of these, it does not mean that it was caused by distress. Some physical symptoms or conditions may be caused by injury or genetics.)

The following StressMap may give you a different perspective.

Body StressMap

	DOES NOT APPLY (N0) 0	BOTHERS ME A LITTLE 1	2	3	4	BOTHERS ME A LOT 5
1. I have difficulty maintaining my correct weight.	0	1	2	3	4	5
2. I have not had enough vacation each year to really be able to physically relax.	0	1	2	3	4	5
3. I find myself tightly gripping a chair or steering wheel or clenching my fists.	0	1	2	3	4	5
4. My hands are cold or clammy at times.	0	1	2	3	4	5
5. I am experiencing muscle tightness or aching in my shoulders.	0	1	2	3	4	5
6. I find myself with clenched or grinding teeth.	0	1	2	3	4	5
7. I have frequent headaches or migraines.	0	1	2	3	4	5
8. I seem to have more frequent colds/viruses/ infections.	0	1	2	3	4	5
9. I tend to feel anxious, nervous, jittery, jumpy.	0	1	2	3	4	5
10. I am exposed in my working or living environment to uncomfortable, irritating a. noises b. temperatures c. vibrations d. air pollutants (dust, smoke, strong odors, chemical vapors, etc.)	0	1	2	3	4	5
11. I have trouble falling asleep or staying asleep.	0	1	2	3	4	5
12. When I do take a vacation or have any free time, I find that I have a hard time relaxing.	0	1	2	3	4	5
13. I drink two or more cups of coffee or tea per day (do not count herbal teas or decaffeinated coffees) (if true, mark 5).	0	1	2	3	4	5
14. I do not engage in some form of enjoyable, aerobic exercise for a minimum of 30 minutes at least three times per week (if true, mark 5).	0	1	2	3	4	5
15. I have three or more alcoholic drinks per week.*	0	1	2	3	4	5
16. I smoke cigarettes, a pipe, cigars, or use smokeless tobacco.	0	1	2	3	4	5

17. I do not use enough quick-release techniques to
    deal with stress (deep muscle relaxation,
    meditation, imagery, body scanning).   0   1   2   3   4   5

* Alcohol, in small amounts, is usually not harmful and, under a physician's direction, can even be helpful in certain situations. However, if alcohol is one of your primary sources of relaxation, reevaluate your stress level and stress relief techniques.

Total your score for body stress (you may find it helpful to refer to the instructions for scoring on page 29).

Total Score:_____

If your score is:

18 or less: Probably dealing effectively with the pressures of body stress.

19 to 54:   This is an area you should examine more closely. Your stress level is high enough that you could in the near future experience some physical or mental signs of distress.

over 54:   Body stress is signaling danger ahead! Please take time now to heed the warning and turn to Chapter 17 Stress Buffers designed for immediate implementation in the area of body stress. Exceeding this level should be a serious warning to you. Don't delay in taking action!

10

Your Life StressMap

*I*t's done! You have six completed StressMaps. Be sure to plot your scores on the next page, "Your Life StressMap." (Pages 54-55.)

No doubt about it, responding to all those statements involved hard work and thoughtful, honest self-analysis — and perhaps even a little stress! Now you are ready to review each StressMap and find out some important information and patterns about the stress you own. The time you spend on this chapter will pay off later in the book, where you will identify and create a stress relief plan to effectively cope with the life stress identify here. It will be a *personal* plan you create to fit *your* needs.

But first, your Life StressMap. Your stress is a unique combination of pressures. As you review each of your six StressMaps, you will benefit most from identifying *patterns* of stress and applying stress management techniques. This approach will reduce or eliminate several stressors, which in turn will reduce other related stressors.

Your stress probably built up over time as a vehicle without brakes builds up speed going downhill. The goal in stress management is to begin a healthy chain reaction to "put on the brakes" in your life and bring it under control.

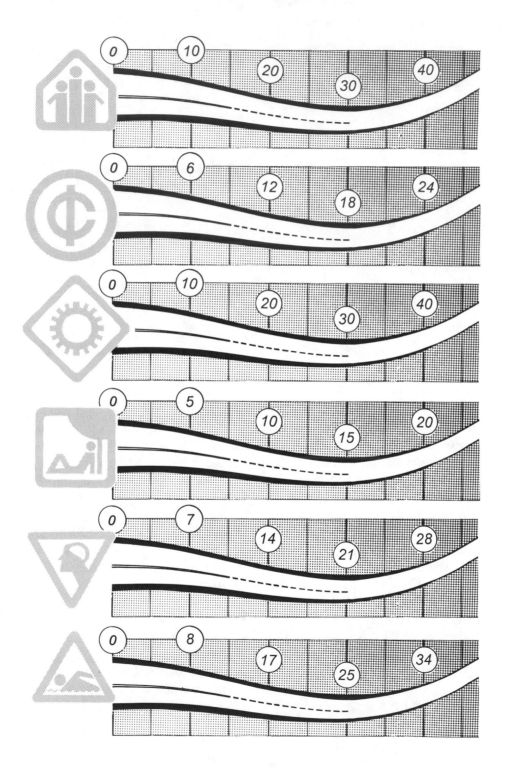

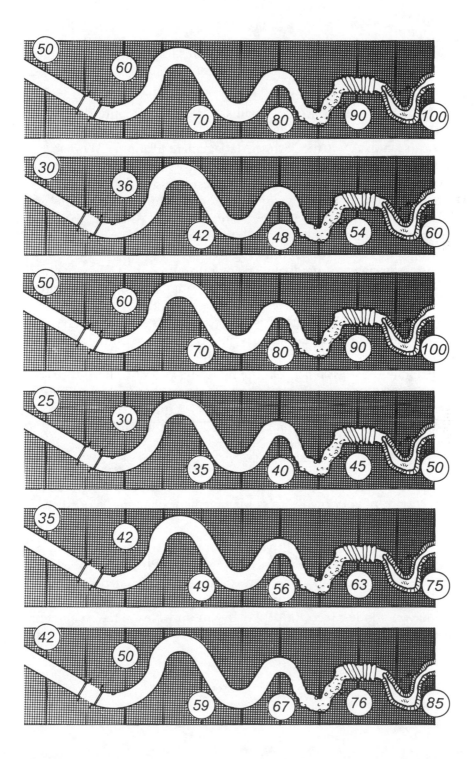

STEP 1

Be sure you have mapped your six scores for stress from Chapters 4-9.

STEP 2

Look at the stress scores for all six areas and identify the two or three areas which have the highest stress (highest scores). List them on the top (section A) of the "Stress Management Planning Worksheet." (Page 60.) Note especially section B, "Patterns." The person shown in the sample worksheet (page 59) had highest stress in the area of Work. With too much to do, there was no time for fun and relaxation. This was reflected in the next highest stress area: Leisure. With no balanced recreation, play or tension-releasing activities, physical problems started surfacing. The result was the third highest stress level: Body.

Stress in one area gradually creeps into other areas. Eventually, if not noticed and relieved, high levels of stress may develop in all six areas of life. The result is *distress*.

No matter what your situation, you are never beyond hope. Whether only one StressMap score is high or all six are off the scale, you can still find relief. Carefully reading the signs along the road to stress is the beginning of stress relief. On the highway, you must heed the signs which say "Reduce Speed Ahead" or "Danger, Road Blocked." Your StressMap scores are your own personal signs. Read them well, understand what they are telling you, and then start doing something specific about stress in your life.

STEP 3

Write a brief note about the patterns you see in your own stress. Use section B of your own "Stress Management Planning Worksheet."

STEP 4

Go back through each of your six area StressMaps in Chapters 4 through 9. In section C of the "Stress Management Planning Worksheet," list *every* statement from all six StressMaps that you rated with a "5." (Section C is the first column of the worksheet.) If you need more space, continue on another piece of paper. If you only have a few statements you rated "5," go back and also list statements you rated with a "4."

Common Life Stress Patterns

* The Social Butterfly
Charlene has without a doubt the most active social calendar in town. President of the PTA, she also belongs to the Garden Club, the Community Beautification Society, the First Church Women's Circle, the County Political Central Committee, and several more groups. She barely sees her family, has not read a book in months, and lives by the clock and the calendar.

* The Workaholic
Fred owns and manages his own business. He has remained successful even in hard economic times by "pure determination and hard work." In the office by 7 a.m., he always takes a briefcase of work home, and spends most evenings at his home computer working out sales projections and financial reports.

* The Hobby Horse
Lorraine has worked with wood since she was a small child watching her grandfather turn out spool beds and chairs on his lathe. She now creates hundreds of small and large objects from wood, carving and shaping for hours, literally forgetting time and other activities. She worries that shortages of fine carving woods will create difficulties for her future projects.

* The StressEater
Howard doesn't enjoy eating; he eats compulsively from habit, boredom, anxiety, even addiction. His food habits center on popular "junk foods," and he abhors anything which has been called "healthy." A chain smoker as well, Howard does not really taste his food, but tends to eat as a ritual.

* The Winner
Joe is a runner. About four years ago, he took up jogging because of its popularity and apparent health value. As he developed strength and capacity to run, he increased his daily jog to twice a day, and gradually doubled his speed. He joined a running club, and entered club contests, working his way up to the annual twenty-six-mile marathon. Last year he won the local event, and this year entered the New York marathon, finishing 103rd in a field of thousands. He now trains six hours each day...

Do any of these life stress patterns remind you of people you know — yourself perhaps?

STEP 5

Review all the stressor statements you have listed. Which statements are *most* stressful, annoying or bothersome? Which would you like to eliminate immediately? Mark these statements with a "1" in section D of the worksheet (the column labeled "Priority Group").

Choose the next most stressful items and rate them with a "2." Continue until you have assigned *all* your 4 and/or 5 stressor statements with a priority rating.

Take your time with this step.

STEP 6

Concentrate on the rankings you gave to your stressors in step 5. What patterns do you see? Make a note in the third (section E) column as to:

- *Who* is involved (yourself, spouse, co-worker)
- *When* the stressors tend to occur (continuously, mornings, on weekends)
- *Where* the stressors are found (on the job, in school, at home)

The person described in the sample worksheet discovered that she was the main person responsible for her own high stress levels. Stress occurred daily, almost continuously on the job but overflowed into all other areas.

STEP 7

As you review your own stressors, priorities, and patterns, note those things that you somehow sense or know intuitively which would probably help your situation. What would you really like to do about your stress? Your insights or ideas may fall into categories like relaxation, physical activity, eating habits, assertiveness, or time management. We'll have more to say about these subjects in later chapters. For now, make a special note of these ideas in the last column (section F). In the next chapter, we will discuss how to convert these items into specific, realistic goals with target dates.

Any time you want to follow a map, you must first find out where you are. Only then can you chart a course to your desired destination. You've just completed that step. Now you know where you are and you have a better understanding about your own stress patterns and how they are related to each other. You also know the "who, when, and where" your stress. And you have established some general goals for change. Using this knowledge to chart a specific course to less stress is the next step.

Sample Stress Management Planning Worksheet

A. HIGHEST STRESS LEVELS

1. work
2. leisure
3. body

B. PATTERNS

Always behind & rushed at work.
Less & less time for leisure (self, family, friends).
Physical problems.

C. STRESSOR STATEMENTS	D. PRIORITY GROUP	E. WHO, WHEN, WHERE?
- I do not engage in some form of strenuous exercise for a minimum of 15 mins. at least 3 times a week	2.	Who? I am responsible for my own stress.
- I feel anxious, nervous, jittery, jumpy	1	When? Everyday almost on a continuous basis.
- I feel my heart racing or pounding daily	3	
- I cannot set limits for myself or stick to them	4	Where? My stress began on the job, but quickly overflowed to home life.
- I have frequent headaches	3	
- More and more I find I need medical care	1	
- When I get to work, I find I need more time	2	

F. GENERAL STRESS MANAGEMENT GOALS AND NOTES

- Improve my time management.
- Get medical help for my nervousness.
- Learn how to relax at work.
- Get help with home chores.
- Notes: relaxation
          time management

Stress Management Planning Worksheet

A. HIGHEST STRESS LEVELS

C. STRESSOR STATEMENTS

D. PRIORITY GROUP

B. PATTERNS

E. WHO, WHEN, WHERE?	F. GENERAL STRESS MANAGEMENT GOALS AND NOTES

11

Life Stress Planning

Relief is on the way! The remaining chapters in this book could be among the most important reading of your life.

Proceed carefully!

At this point you have some important information about stress in your life. You know you're an "owner" of stress. You know which of your six StressMaps are the most distressful. You also know the major people, places and times involved in your stress. Now you're ready to go to work on the changes you'll make to *relieve* your stress.

Your Life StressMap is one-of-a-kind; stress itself is very personalized, reflecting your lifestyle. In the same way, a stress relief plan must be designed to fit your unique needs. While no two relief plans are exactly alike, each, if it is to be effective, should incorporate these six basic stress relief tools:

1. POSITIVE BELIEFS

Your mind and what it believes is the most important aspect of effective stress management. In Chapter 3 we provided you several examples of how your beliefs, hopes, attitudes and expectations can create either your dreams or your worst fears. The message you will want to remember is that your mind is yours and it creates only what you allow it to create. We hope you will use the resources of this book to create the dreams, the reality you want.

2. RELAXATION AND BREATHING

These two simple, free techniques are skills you can easily learn that will create positive changes in your body and will reverse the effects of distress. You will want to have the ability to relax the muscles in your body, anywhere, when you begin to feel tension and pressure. Without this skill, distress gradually builds over weeks and months until something drastic happens which forces a slowing down. Relaxation, when linked to deep rhythmic breathing, is a free, quick, calming, and refreshing activity — the alternative to physical and psychological difficulties and the helplessness and anguish that usually accompany them. Chapter 18 will teach you specific skills in how to relax.

3. HEALTHY EATING HABITS

In many ways, "your stress is what you eat." Stress relief through nutrition doesn't mean severe fasting, complete abstinence from everything prepackaged, or expensive health foods. We advocate an understanding of nutritional basics and a common sense approach to your eating habits. We also urge a gradual change of eating habits as you adapt and learn more about what you put in your body. We suggest that you make eating a part of your overall program of stress management while you make it an adventure in discovery. Chapter 19 begins the adventure.

4. PHYSICAL ACTIVITY

It's play! For a child, play is pure enjoyment, with freedom and exhilaration mixed in. Do you remember? Finding your own play activities and letting yourself enjoy them regularly is a powerful mental and physical stress relief. Chapter 20 is a start to finding your play.

5. TIME MANAGEMENT

This is a very useful tool to keep time from controlling and terrorizing you and adding more distress. Satisfaction, accomplishment, peace of mind, and control can result when you hone your time management skills to produce relief from distress. Chapter 21 provides lots of tips.

6. ASSERTIVENESS

Assertive behavior contributes to control of your life without causing you distress or creating it in others. Effective self-assertion is another very important skill to develop. Stress relief depends in part on being assertive — able to express yourself and your needs without pushing others around.

Your next step is to decide how you will adapt these general stress management techniques to fit your individual situation. As you develop plans, you must be sure that you *want* to work on them and that you can *realistically* accomplish them. Every goal must also be stated very carefully in *specific* terms. Review the six goal-setting criteria and the examples on pages 26 and 27.

Look at the sample "Stress Management Plan" below. The stress management program for this individual would require approximately three hours each week to gain better control. Gaining better control over the workload will produce more leisure time which, carefully used, will result in a healthier body.

Sample Stress Management Plan

A. GENERAL GOALS AND AREAS OF NOTE	B. PRIORITY GROUP	C. SPECIFIC STRESS MANAGEMENT PLANS
-Improve my time management.	2	Time Management 1- Make better work plans every morning
-get medical help for my nervousness.	1	2 - Delegate at work & at home
-get help with home chores	3	3 -Evaluate time & energy for any new project
-Notes: relaxation time mgt.		Relaxation 1- Do neck-stretching exercises every hour at work 2- Do 15 min relaxing exercise at lunch. Physical Fitness 1- Start Jazzercise 2- Take 5 min.walk at lunchtime

Now refer back to your own "Stress Management Planning Worksheet" on pages 60 and 61. In section F, you wrote some general goals for yourself. This is the time to translate those general goals into written, specific, realistic goals with target dates and support. Use the Stress Management Plan on page 67, the procedures noted above, and the sample Stress Management Plan (on page 65) as guides. Add goals you did not identify in Chapter 10, but be sure to make them very specific at this time. You are developing a plan for action now, and it must be made up of steps you can accomplish!

As you think about your goals, it will help to examine the "Stress Buffers" chapters for ideas and leads. Become a real Sherlock Holmes: one of the ideas in a chapter may lead you to read a book which may be the key to helping you cope more with a particular stress pattern. Take a little extra time to investigate thoroughly; you owe it to yourself!

Stress management skills, like eating, sleeping and breathing, are necessities of life. You need them all on a *regular* basis to remain healthy. You undoubtedly have modified your eating and sleeping habits at different points in your life to fit your changing needs. The same should be true for stress management techniques. They must become a permanent part of your lifestyle if you are to achieve and maintain high level wellness and eustressful living.

Enjoy yourself as you design your own stress relief program, and commit it to writing by using the "Stress Management Plan" format provided here.

It takes courage to let go of stress, and it can be scary to take control of your life. That's what the remainder of this book offers: control through stress relief. In many ways changing your life begins with being assertive with yourself. Decide to follow your plan, and start your adventure in stress relief.

The next six chapters offer "Stress Buffers" — short-term suggestions for immediate response to the six areas of life stress you have mapped. They will help you over immediate day-to-day stress hurdles.

Chapters 18 to 21 provide greater depth of assistance in the relaxation, physical activity, eating habits, and time management.

Now it's time to complete your personal Stress Management Plan. When you have your Plan, your next step is to begin to put it into practice!

Stress Management Plan

A. GENERAL GOALS AND AREAS OF NOTE (from Chapter 10)	B. PRIORITY GROUP	C. SPECIFIC STRESS MANAGEMENT PLANS

12

People Stress Buffers

*L*et's get started doing something about your stress! The short list of suggestions in this chapter will give you lots of ideas for immediate action you can take to combat your "people stress." None of the *stress buffers* is intended as a long-range answer to the people stress in your life, but every one of them offers a step you can take *now* — today, tomorrow, this week — toward reducing distress. Find two or three that fit your situation and try them out.

Do Unto Others...

How would you like it if someone were kind and compassionate to you just because you are you? Consider thinking more and more about others and how *you* as one person can make a difference. A wonderful small book that can give you delightful ideas is *Guerrilla Kindness* by Gavin Whitsett. Here are a couple of examples:...

> * The station manager at our public radio station makes staff meetings more fun by putting "Hero Of The Week" at the top of the agenda. She picks a different staffer each week, acknowledges a specific good thing the person has done over the last week, and gives him or her the Hero award to keep on display for seven days.

> *April and Todd take *Guerrilla Kindness* to the streets. They leave quarters in soda and candy machines along with stick-on notes: "Have one on us ... and pass it on! The Kindness Guerrillas."

Smile

Analyze what makes you smile, and make a real effort to smile more often. Maybe it is an old Peter Sellers movie, "Saturday Night Live" on television, an article by Art Buchwald, or a comic strip like Garfield. Take the time to help yourself smile.

Develop Hobbies or Interests

If you find yourself dissatisfied with life in general, it may be time to develop some new interests or hobbies, or perhaps something as risky as a career change or a return to school for further training. Potential hobbies or pastimes can be done alone or with others. They don't have to cost much (or any) money either.

Rebuild After Your Divorce/Separation

The crisis of divorce or separation brings about new and frightening circumstances in your life which forces you into new routines, new behaviors, and a lot of distress. Many community organizations, such as churches and colleges, sponsor groups dealing with the emotions involved in this grieving process. Another resource would be an excellent book: *Rebuilding* by Bruce Fisher.

Allow Yourself To Grieve

If there has been a recent loss of someone important to you, consider joining a group to help you deal with your feelings. Also, you might find helpful some books by Elisabeth Kubler-Ross: *On Death and Dying* and *Death: The Final Stage of Growth*.

Cut Back Television

If you find that you are spending too much time in front of the television, consider moving it to a less accessible location in the house. Visit your local library and check out some "best sellers" and place them in strategic reading locations like the bedroom and bathroom. The chapter on Leisure has a few other ideas on the television.

Become Assertive

Learn responsible assertive behavior which will allow you to increase your personal effectiveness. Being assertive means standing up for your personal rights and expressing your feelings, thoughts, and opinions in a direct, honest, and appropriate way which does not violate another's personal rights.

Remember E.U. Stress and D.I. Stress back in Chapter 3? "D.I." was the person who couldn't handle the late alarm clock, and had trouble all day as a result. "E.U." took it pretty much in stride, and managed a productive day anyway. Several of the steps "E.U." took to help deal with the situation could be called *assertive* actions.

You may already consider yourself to be assertive in most situations. Nevertheless, we urge you to give the material in this section careful attention, especially if your People Stress score (Chapter 4) is above 33.

Unresolved problems which nag and bother, such as D.I. Stress experienced, often result in increased tension — and more and more anxiety. If put off, something that would have been easy to handle may grow in seriousness and get out of hand. Resolving such problems early can allow greater enjoyment of other activities and leisure, and assertiveness is a big help.

All of us are assertive to some degree; we may be able to say what we feel, to be open, honest, direct and respectful of others' feelings. In other situations, we may allow *others* to make decisions for us, or even to violate our own rights. This is *non-assertive* behavior. At other times it can be too easy to speak out without regard for others' feelings. This is *aggressive* behavior. Learning the differences among these three types of behavior (assertive, non-assertive, and aggressive) and in what situations to use each is a key in making life more eustressful.

Later in this section you will find a list of everyday situations which call for assertive action. As you read each, consider your own behavior under similar conditions. Such a self-examination will give you an idea of the types of situations in which you may choose to be more assertive, and therefore guide your improvement efforts.

The next step toward more eustressful living is to *be* more assertive. You can grow in this area through classes and workshops, or with the help of a number of excellent books. The "Suggested Readings" section lists several of the more helpful books on the subject.

Assertive behavior can appear deceptively simple, of course. We suggest, "Be assertive!" as if you could go right out and change your life. Actually, the process is more complex than that. It does take practice, and sometimes guidance from a qualified professional trainer and/or a comprehensive self-help book. We suggest you check out *any* assertiveness training program to be sure it offers help — or referral — in four areas:

. . .*attitudes and thoughts*. Your belief system, ways
of looking at life, and thoughts about yourself are
important elements of your personal effectiveness.

. . .behavioral skills. Do you listen well? Do you look at others while talking? Do you stand erect? How is your timing? These skills and others can make all the difference!

. . .anxiety. Anxiety and tension can prevent or distort effective communication, even if your attitudes and skills are right on target.

. . .external obstacles. Many life circumstances inhibit assertion. It's tougher to be firm with a boss when jobs are scarce, for example.

Achieving greater control in your life is a key dimension of stress management. Even if you consider yourself assertive already, there may be specific areas of your life which cause you difficulty and stress. We encourage you to read at least one of the recommended books on assertive behavior, and consider its potential value in helping to reduce your stress.

Assertiveness in Everyday Situations

- If a couple near me in a theater or at a lecture were conversing loudly, I would say something to them.
- If a salesperson has gone to considerable trouble to show me merchandise which is not quite suitable, I still say "no."
- I like to learn new games and skills.
- I am comfortable talking to attractive persons of the opposite sex.
- If a famed and respected lecturer made a statement that I thought was incorrect, I would share my view with the audience.
- I am comfortable making phone calls to businesses and institutions.
- I am open and frank in expressing my feelings.
- If something I buy is not suitable, I return it.
- When I do something important or worthwhile, I share my feelings of pride with others.
- If I knew someone was spreading false stories about me, I would talk to that person about it.
- I complain when I get poor service or bad food in a restaurant.
- I ask friends to do favors for me.
- I express my feelings even when it may "make a scene."
- I am comfortable starting conversations with new acquaintances and strangers.

- If a friend borrowed $10 from me and forgot about it, I would remind the person to pay me back.
- I am comfortable asking questions in a group or class.
- When someone asks me to do something that I don't want to do, I say "no."
- I consider my own feelings equally important to those of others.
- I am able to enjoy rest and leisure.
- I know my needs are as important as the needs of other people.
- I consider making mistakes alright.
- I can ask for information from others, especially professionals.

Make Chores More Fun

Try some new ideas for some monotonous everyday chores. Enroll in a cooking class for some new recipes, or check out some cookbooks from the public library. Set aside one day a week (or at least one night a week) just for fun. The chapter on Leisure has some good suggestions. Try car pooling or riding a bike to work. Make household duties a family/children undertaking. The Leisure chapter has some ideas on rewards that would also apply here.

Enjoy Meals

Meals can be a family time, not just additional television time. In most families, meals provide one of the only times when everyone is together at the same time; it's a great opportunity for nurturing the family spirit as well as the individual bodies. We urge that emphasis be placed on increasing the pleasantness and the quality of this time. Make meals a time when everyone can share positive experiences of the day.

Hold Family Councils

Once-a-week meetings for the whole family provide a special opportunity to discuss those situations which are going to cause some changes or decisions to be made for the whole family. Items for discussion might include vacation plans, household chores, budgeting, etc. Anyone over six years of age can be expected to participate. The meeting should not deteriorate into a "gripe" or "preaching" session, but should provide an opportunity to express ideas and feelings and experience a respectful cooperation among everyone present. A book describing this process is *Family Council* by Dr. Rudolph Dreikurs, Shirley Gould and Dr. Raymond Corsini.

Handle Children's Misbehavior Constructively

No children are perfect; there are times when they actually misbehave! In dealing with children, and making parent survival easier, you might want to consider the following thoughts.

- Parents and children should share mutual respect; neither adult nor child should take advantage of the other.
- A child is nurtured by encouragement just as a plant is by water.
- Punishment should be based on natural consequences. A child needs to be "protected" from these consequences only in times of danger. Obviously you wouldn't allow a child to experience the "natural consequences" of running into a busy street or playing with matches.
- When your clearly and firmly stated words fail to gain the response you want from your child, take action. Remember your child can tune you out just as well as you can tune out the child. Base your conversations with your child on friendliness, mutual respect and love. Do not discipline with verbal threats. Do not try to converse in times of conflict. It is inevitable that you will say or do something you will later regret. Perhaps withdrawing from the scene of conflict is the most effective action.
- Forego trying to create a dependent child. Encourage the child to develop his/her own abilities. It might take more time, but the child will learn to be more responsible.
- Try to understand the reason behind your child's misbehavior. Remember that the child is trying to gain social status, even though the child's goals may be misdirected (attention-getting, power, revenge or display of inadequacy).

Learn Effective Parenting/Stepparenting Skills

Another avenue for consideration is updating or acquiring more appropriate parenting skills. It is a foregone conclusion that no one ever teaches us to be parents, so there should be no embarrassment in claiming ignorance.

Many community colleges and school districts offer "parent effectiveness" courses. You might also consider acquiring a book describing exceptional parenting skills. One good book on the subject is *Raising a Responsible Child* by Dr. Don Dinkmeyer and Gary D. McKay.

Let Children Share Housework

Children and housework does not have to be a source of conflict. They can be helpful partners in this responsibility if you follow some simple guidelines:

- teach your child to do the task
- accept the fact that a child may not be able to do the task like you or another adult (accept less than perfection)
- start your child at a young age in sharing the housework responsibilities
- appropriately reward the child for helping (rewards do not have to cost money and should include sincere verbal praise)
- consider letting the child select the task or give the child a task appropriate for his or her physical abilities (this will minimize frustration and encourage future participation)
- teach the child to have fun doing the task

Plan Family Vacations

Engage all family members in your efforts to decide on a vacation site or activity that everyone can enjoy. Be sure that each family member can have his/her share in the decision-making process. Use a family council meeting or two to air everybody's ideas.

De-stress Your Child

Children learn from adults who teach them through instructions and modeling of behavior. You can help your child grow up to be a more effective manager of distress. Consider the following tips:

- set a good example in eating, relaxing, breathing, assertiveness, conflict management, having fun, praying and other positive habits
- monitor and restrict television, video and movie viewing
- try not to overreact to some rebelliousness as the child grows through the developmental stages
- help your child to express feelings by listening and rephrasing without judging
- minimize pressure by accepting the child's limitations (physical and mental) and by helping the child to refrain from pressuring him or herself
- sincerely and frequently acknowledge and celebrate the child's accomplishments (it helps to be a part of the accomplishments by attending events or helping the child with a task if appropriate)

- model respect for the child, for yourself and for others. Help the child be loving to him- or herself, to others and to animals
- be honest when answering questions
- try not to compare and discourage the child from comparing him- or herself to others
- seek professional help if you need assistance with a problem

Nurture a Friendship

Everyone needs a confidante or a good friend. Cultivate or rekindle such a relationship, and risk sharing your emotions and feelings. You will most likely find the risk worthwhile.

Do It Yourself

Consider repairing a car, a small appliance, a piece of furniture or other items with a friend and a how-to book from the library, and you may find that the companionship is as rewarding as the new skill you may learn.

Cook

Call up a friend each week, and ask him or her for a favorite recipe; then try it!

Try New Things with Friends and Lovers

- Purchase five or six romantic greeting cards all at once. Write special thoughts and leave them in a different place every week or so.
- Spread a blanket in the living room. Have a wine, cheese, and fruit picnic while listening to your favorite music. Forget about the time and concentrate on the person who is with you.
- When that special one is working intensely for long hours, give him or her a loving two-minute neck and shoulder massage.
- Have supper prepared when she/he walks in the door. This is especially appreciated when it is not your scheduled night to cook.
- Plan a small (or big) "YOU ARE LOVED" party. Invite your friend or lover's special friends. Have each bring his / her favorite verse or poem which expresses a special feeling.
- Rekindle a relationship by planning a quiet evening where the two of you share memories, photos or old letters from your relationship.
- Make a list of all the strengths and positive points you see and like in your special one. Write three or four at a time on small notes and leave them in different spots at different but regular

intervals. Say it simply such as: "I like you because you are (list the strengths). To be continued...."
- Save a little money here and there until you have enough to give your special one the cash to spend only on him or herself.
- Spend an evening lying on a blanket watching for shooting stars while sipping a favorite drink.
- Offer to do the laundry, lawn, shopping or any other chore if your partner uses the extra time to relax.
- Enroll both of you in an activity you both enjoy or would like to learn (dancing, ceramics, wine tasting, gourmet cooking, stained glass, exercise...).
- Buy a plant or flower arrangement. (It will mean even more if it is not for a special occasion.) Many men find this especially meaningful!
- Buy an album of relaxing special effects, like ocean waves or a forest stream. Have a living room picnic with the background sounds.
- Set aside an hour on a regular basis (at least once a week) to share memories, experiences, thoughts, dreams, ideas. Sometimes it helps to preselect the topic.
- Give a body massage by candlelight using incense, lotions, body paints, vibrators, or whatever else pleases. Make a massage a *regular* happening.
- Do tasks or chores together. Talk while you are working. It's amazing how enjoyable work can become and how fast it seems to get done.
- Select a theme such as vacations, your future together, a special occasion from your past, a shared dream, dating mementos. Collect photos, magazine pictures, and quotes. Spend an hour or two a month making a collage together.
- Pick a weekend or even a full week and switch chores around the house. Talk about how it felt over a relaxing meal.
- Before the weekends arrive, spend a few minutes together planning some special time together. This is especially important if one or both of you have a tendency to work away the weekend.

You should have the idea now! Be creative; dream up your own thoughtful and fun ways to increase your friendship or deepen your love.

People Bibliography
(Note "Children and Parents" section on next page)

Alberti, *Making Yourself Heard: A Guide to Assertive Relationships*

Alberti and Emmons, *Your Perfect Right: A Guide to Assertive Living*

Beckfield, *Master Your Panic...and Take Back Your Life!: Twelve Treatment Sessions to Overcome High Anxiety*

Bricklin, Golin, and Grandinetti, *Positive Living and Health: The Complete Guide to Brain/Body Healing and Mental Empowerment*

Campbell, *Beyond the Power Struggle: Dealing with Conflict in Love and Work*

Dreikurs, Gould, and Corsini, *Family Council*

Emmons and Alberti, *Accepting Each Other: Individuality and Intimacy in Your Loving Relationship*

Fisher, *Rebuilding: When Your Relationship Ends*

Frankl, *Man's Search for Meaning*

Heath, *Long Distance Caregiving: A Survival Guide for Far Away Caregivers*

Kubler-Ross, *Death: The Final Stage of Growth*

Kubler-Ross, *On Death and Dying*

Lange and Jakubowski, *Responsible Assertive Behavior*

Peck, *A World Waiting to be Born: Civility Rediscovered*

Powell, *The Secret of Staying in Love*

Powell, *Why Am I Afraid to Love?*

Whitsett, *Guerrilla Kindness: A Manual of Good Works, Kind Acts, and Thoughtful Deeds*

For a more complete description of these books, please see "Suggested Readings," page 179.

Children and Parents

Dinkmeyer and McKay, *Raising a Responsible Child*

Elkind, *All Grown Up and No Place to Go: Teenagers in Crisis*

Gordon, *Parent Effectiveness Training*

Gregg, and Boston Children's Medical Center Staff, *What to Do When There's Nothing to Do*

Kuzma, *Prime-Time Parenting*

Munsch, *Love You Forever*

Palmer, *"I Wish I Could Hold Your Hand...": A Child's Guide to Grief and Loss*

Palmer, *Liking Myself*

Palmer, *Teen Esteem: A Self-Direction Manual for Young Adults*

Palmer, *The Mouse, the Monster and Me*

Saunders, *The Stress-Proof Child: A Loving Parent's Guide*

Thornburg, *The Bubblegum Years: Sticking with Kids from 9-13*

Vollbracht, *The Way of the Circle*

Williams, *Cool Cats, Calm Kids*

For a more complete description of these books, please see
"Suggested Readings," page 179.

13

Money Stress Buffers

*T*he short list of suggestions in this chapter will give you lots of ideas for immediate action you can take to combat your "money stress." None of the *stress buffers* is intended as a long-range answer to the money stress in your life, but every one of them offers a step you can take *now* — today, tomorrow, this week — toward reducing distress. Find two or three that fit your situation and try them out.

Take Control

The initial step in overcoming money stress is taking control. Planning, goal setting and record-keeping may sound like work, but if you're going to manage your money well, they are essential. You never get anywhere unless you know where you have been. And the longer you wait, the more difficult it will be to reach your goals, no matter what they are. You want to get the most out of what you are bringing home in that paycheck.

Make a Plan

You will want to actively plan for those things you want to see happen in the future. Whether it is *long-range goals* — retirement, a mountain home, college education for your children — or more modest *short-range goals* — this year's vacation, a new car — or just handling *current income and expenses* more effectively, the plan brings you closer today to where you want to be tomorrow. This is a process of realizing your dreams. Isn't this one of the major reasons you are working today?

Lay out all your financial obligations so that your picture is complete. Many people hesitate to do this because they are afraid of what they might find out. However, you might be in better shape than you thought.

Write It Down

When you have decided what your goals are then be sure to go to the next step and write them down. It is a bit too late to decide how you are going to finance that college education, once your child is graduating from high school. You can separate your goals into three distinct categories: short-range: taking place within the next twelve months, medium-range: what you hope to achieve within the next five years and lastly, long-range: what you envision in the next fifteen to twenty years. After you have come to agreements with yourself, post your goals in prominent places: refrigerator door, bathroom mirror. These will serve as constant reminders during the difficult times. If you are really serious about making your money goals — or *any* goals — a reality, ask someone who is committed to your best interests to support you in achieving your goals. Be specific in how this special person can help you.

Put Your Brain in Charge of Your Money — Not Your Heart

Emotions play a large part in the waste of money. Comments like "I owe it to myself," "Nothing is too good for my kids," "I know I can't afford it, but...," "This is a one-in-a-lifetime opportunity," "It probably won't be there the next time," lead to trouble and overspending. You need to march yourself out the door and stay away until the urge passes. You also need to lay out how much these goals will cost you so you do know how much to save monthly.

Ask for Budget Plans

Many companies including utility companies are willing to put you on a twelve-month average schedule so that there are no surprises from heat in the winter or air conditioning in the summer. With these plans you can count on the same amount of money required monthly to cover these debits.

Keep Phone Bills in Check

These bills can be astronomical especially if you have a teenager in the house. Since telephone companies have become so competitive, shop around to be sure you have the best deal for your lifestyle. And remember, postcards are cheaper than phone calls!

Choose Recreation over Entertainment

Once you get into the chapter on physical fitness you will realize that recreation is not only healthier than entertainment — it's cheaper! Another reason to be physically fit!

Multiply Spending Control by Dividing Your Accounts

You might consider giving yourself two checking accounts. One account into which your check will be deposited and that you will use to pay for all major purchases or bills and another one that can be a personal or surplus account. This might help you with that needed control over spending. You might also consider having two savings account. One can take care of unexpected bills and the other can handle those goals that you have. Some banks allow you to open an account just for Christmas spending. That prevents you from feeling that you are not going to make it through December and January, since the money has already been saved ahead of time.

Watch the Road Ahead

There are signs that will let you know that there are rough times ahead. Be aware so again you can be prepared. These signs include times when you find it necessary to use money out of your savings account to pay for monthly expenses, delaying payments that you use to pay promptly, charging everyday expenses and taking more than one year to pay off outstanding debts(outside of your house and car). If this is happening to you, you need to be ready to make some cuts.

Do It Yourself

It is sometimes cheaper to fix what you have before you make the decision to buy new. "Do it yourself" and "tune-up" classes are probably available in your community and can save you when it come to costly maintenance for the family car. Similar opportunities exist in home landscaping, furniture refinishing, small appliance repair, clothing construction and more.

Shop Smart

Be sure that you have a shopping list before you walk into a grocery store. You will be sure that you don't forget items and you will eliminate impulse buying which costs you more.

Work with Creditors

If you can't make it to the end of the month and cannot meet your obligations, be sure and visit with your creditors. Work with them to establish a new schedule of payments. Above all, protect your credit!

Use Consolidation Loans Cautiously

These loans can work very well if you are making several payments on installment loans. Even if you reduce your payments to one, however, do not take on additional debt until you have paid this one off. And check the interest rates carefully! Some advertised consolidation loans are at *very* high interest. It won't help you to have only one payment if you wind up paying hundreds (or thousands) of dollars more in interest over the long run!

Make a Money Workspace

Create a space where bills can be collected and your finances maintained. It is important and you need to make space for it. There is nothing worse than looking in drawers and cardboard boxes for records and paperwork that need to be right at hand.

Keep Payments on Schedule

To be sure that your major bills (like the mortgage and the car) are paid in a timely fashion, you may consider using devices such as automatic payroll deductions or transfers from your checking or saving accounts.

Put Needs Ahead of Wants

Be sure that your needs have been paid off before you start to even consider your wants. In other words, you are old enough not to let your wants hurt you. We do realize that wants are important. Are they important enough for you to put away even a small amount every month to acquire something in several months?

Shrink Credit Card Debt

At their best credit cards are a convenience for travel and short-term purchases. Keep your credit cards to a minimum and don't expand your credit just because your income does. The more credit cards that you have in your wallet, the more the temptation to spend. Never, never charge everyday expenses (e.g., groceries, utility bills). Substitute a debit card for the use of a credit card. You will not have any interest charges and you can also keep within your established budget. You have the convenience without the temptation. Because of their very high interest rates, it's important not to use credit cards to charge amounts greater than you can pay off at the end of the month. If you need a *loan,* negotiate for the best terms available — don't use your cards! If you have credit card debt, *pay it off as quickly as possible.* If you pay just the minimum payment, interest will continue to pile up on the remaining balance and you'll never get it paid off. It may help to recognize the reality of unpaid credit cards: "sale" items are really very expensive purchases when you consider the interest you pay over months (hopefully not years). Maybe if you feel cheated, even by yourself, you might not charge as much.

Get Help

You might want to consider hiring a professional in the financial field to give you some insight. This assistance can be a good investment but remember to do your homework before hiring someone, check references and talk to satisfied customers. There is also free credit counseling available in most states. Look in the telephone book under Consumer Credit Counseling.

Avoid Addiction

You can become addicted to spending just like tobacco or alcohol. You can identify a number of psychological reasons for the high spending money can give you and for some this may become chronic. If you need help you can contact your local chapter of Debtors' Anonymous, a support program patterned after alcoholics' anonymous.

Put Your Spending in Perspective

A great many people live on less than you do. If you spent money the way they do, you could save and invest the difference.

Plan Your Grocery Shopping

You might consider joining those stores which allow you to buy in bulk for wholesale prices. There are savings plus when you buy in bulk you reduce the number of times you need to visit the grocery store, more savings because you won't be tempted by impulses. Develop a family food plan which compares economical, low-cost, moderate-cost and liberal plans. The US Department of Agriculture has many suggestions (Washington, DC 20250). Ask them for a list of their pamphlets.

Eat Out Wisely

When you choose to eat out, choose healthy and frugal. Consider vegetarian, its cheaper, not to mention healthier. Forget beverages, including alcohol (there is a tremendous markup), and go for water; it's also healthier! Think of eating out as a luxury you should limit.

Get Out of Your Car

Consider other forms of transportation like bus systems or light rail if available in your community. Consider car pooling. Commuter passes might save you some money as well. If you need to drive, find a car that's financially manageable. Sell those extra cars that hang around your driveway. You can only drive one at a time.

Don't Get Lost in the Medical Marketplace

Medical expenses often snow people under and place them in desperate situations in times of crisis. In order to reduce the prolonged effect, consider the following ideas:

- Secure a primary care physician while you are well, and therefore have an opportunity to do some comparative shopping before the need arises.
- If a stay in the hospital is inevitable, do without a private room. Also talk over with your doctor the possibility of choosing the hospital. Sometimes you will find differences in charges.
- Request generic brand prescriptions.
- Keep updated medical insurance.
- Keep records on your medical expenses since they are tax deductions.
- Don't abuse your insurance or managed care benefits. Costs are going up too fast already; we don't need unnecessary premium hikes!

Save Raises

If you get a raise, consider having all or part of it sent automatically to a savings account or credit union. It is an excellent way to start and then continue a savings program before getting used to the extra money. We know at least one colleague who put himself through graduate school on savings from his raises during the preceding four years.

Don't Worry, Be Happy

Be happy with what you have and don't continually yearn for those things that you do not have and cannot afford right now.

Potpourri

- *Idea:* Have a "home energy efficiency audit." Your local public utilities service probably offers it at no cost. Then do the recommended upgrading yourself.
- *Idea:* Share day care and/or baby-sitting with friends or neighbors. Do not exchange money, just time.
- *Idea:* Try vacations that are shorter and closer to home. There are probably great places to see in a fifty mile radius around your home.
- *Idea:* Save by using low-cost, hair-cutting salons.
- *Idea:* Encourage your older children to seek jobs so they can help out with a few of their own needs or wants.

•*Idea:* Cultivate interests that are low-cost. Seeing friends, reading, walking, or hiking can be good for your finances as well as your health.

•*Idea:* Entertainment can be less costly if you look for those times and days that have discount prices.

•*Idea:* Have a regular garage sale.

•*Idea:* Initiate a "white elephant" gift exchange with friends and family members. Just remember who gave who what.

•*Idea:* Try making your gifts. You can't help stumbling across ideas in the popular magazines. Do it as a family, and save money in the process.

•*Idea:* Shop for quality — products that will last — rather than price alone.

Money Bibliography

Ackerman, *Getting Rich*

Briles, *The Woman's Guide to Financial Savvy*

Moe, *Making Your Paycheck Last*

Perkins and Rhoades, *The Women's Financial Survival Handbook*

Tyson, *Personal Finance for Dummies*

VanCaspel, *Money Dynamics for the 1990's*

For a more complete description of these books, please see "Suggested Readings," page 179.

14

Work Stress Buffers

*T*he short list of suggestions in this chapter will give you lots of ideas for immediate action you can take to combat your "work stress." None of the *stress buffers* is intended as a long-range answer to the work stress in your life, but every one of them offers a step you can take *now* — today, tomorrow, this week — toward reducing distress. Find two or three that fit your situation and try them out.

Nurture Relationships
Make an effort to seek out colleagues and form rewarding, pleasant, and cooperative relationships. Review Chapter 12 for ideas.

Prioritize
Be realistic about *how much* you can handle on the job and learn to manage the priorities. A good reference is Lakein's *How to Get Control of Your Time and Your Life*, especially Chapter IV, "Control Starts with Planning." See also Chapter 21 in *this* book.

Set Target Dates
Set target dates for completion of every project. If your boss sets deadlines for you, suggest to him / her that you set them together. If this seems impossible, check the references in "Prioritize" above.

Take Control
Plan ahead for possible crises and deadlines, and anticipate your own action. The secret is taking control of your life.

Relax Briefly - 1

Take time out from your schedule (if only for five minutes) several times a day and relax. When possible, move around. Get up from your work station or do some stretching in place if you can't leave for a few minutes. Mentally detach yourself from the job for a few minutes and use pleasant scenes or thoughts to revitalize yourself. Another technique you might want to try: Become aware when your breathing is shallow and fast. When this does happen, briefly stop what you are doing and analyze what you are doing, thinking and feeling. Take control and breathe more slowly and more deeply. This will help reduce those feelings of anxiety. (See also Chapter 18.)

Relax Briefly - 2

Instead of taking six seconds and popping an aspirin or Valium, try using the same six seconds and relax for free. It is a simple three-step process, each step taking just two seconds. Step one: Stop what you're doing and take a long, slow, deep breath. Step two: Smile sincerely as you slowly begin exhaling. Step three: As you continue to exhale, relax your body, beginning with your shoulders, while mentally saying something to yourself such as "I'm relaxing."

Relax Briefly - 3

Another six second freebie. You may like it and try it for more than six seconds. Step one: place your elbows on a table. Step two: lightly touch your first three fingertips to your forehead above each eyebrow. Step three: hold this position for at least four seconds, while breathing slowly and thinking positive about yourself and your situation. In seconds you will, amazingly, feel waves of relaxation flowing through your body.

Take Mental Time Outs

Make a conscious effort to relax yourself prior to a presentation, meeting, or important phone call. Remember to breathe.

Take Walks

Take a walk (even for only five minutes) to keep your body refreshed, relaxed and alert. Make it pleasant and greet people you meet along the way. Don't forget to smile (sincerely!) and breathe.

Cut Out the Noise

Check out the noise level of your work area. Be creative in finding ways of reducing it. Noise is a big contributor to distress.

Schedule Interruptible Time

Schedule specific times that you *will permit interruptions*. Consider returning all phone calls half an hour before lunch and half an hour before closing. People generally are not interested in carrying on long discourses at these times of day.

Avoid Overtime

Do not spend eight straight hours in your office or workplace if you can avoid it. No eating over your desk or staying that extra half hour after quitting time, either!

Keep Meetings on Time

Begin meetings at unusual times (9:47, 2:09) for variety. Announce when the meeting will end and stick to that schedule. Ask someone to be a timekeeper for you if it will help you.

Hold Meetings on The Hoof

If the meeting is to be very short, consider asking everybody to stand.

Cut Telephone Small Talk

Begin business telephone conversations with the reason you called. Not "How are you?" or "What's new?"

Cope Now

Deal with distressful problems immediately. It is better to deal with short-term distress instead of letting it become long-term anxiety, discomfort or illness.

Worry Later

Take control of your problems and worries. Periodically make a *worry list*.* Write down the problems that concern you and beside each one write down what you are going to do. It is easier to deal with problems once they are in the open.

---

* From Karl Albrecht, *Stress and the Manager*. Adapted with permission of Prentice- Hall, Inc.

Box Your Worries

You do it. We do it. We would bet even the publisher of this book does it. While worrying is rather common place, it is not something you have to accept as a burden in your life. In addition to writing down your worries, which gets them out of your head where your mind will create big monsters, try dropping each worry into one of the four categories or boxes in the diagram below and see what happens to them when you shed some reality on them.

I can control *Important to me* Do something about your worries that fall in this category	*I CANNOT control* *Important to me* Why waste your time on worries over which you have no control?
I can control *NOT important to me* Why waste your time on worries that are not important to you (unless they are "dictated" to you)?	*I CANNOT control* *NOT important to me* Worst category of time wasters for you!! Think about your worries that fall into this category!

Be Assertive

Say what you feel. Be assertive: open, honest, direct, but don't consciously hurt the other person. You violate your own rights (and hurt yourself) if you act non-assertively. You violate others' rights (and hurt them) if you are aggressive. Learning the differences among the three types of behavior and how to incorporate more assertive behaviors into your life is possible through assertiveness training. The result can produce less stress not only on the job but throughout your life. More in Chapter 12.

Be Ready for Career Changes

Stress may be so overwhelming for you that a change in your work environment may be the only solution. This could be either a change in the present job (by revising job descriptions or shifting positions), or a completely new job with a new organization. Even if a job change is not in your immediate future, it may not be far away. Most American workers will change careers several times during their work life. Be prepared by keeping your skills updated and your resume current. An excellent book is available that can help you be as prepared as possible: *What Color is Your Parachute?* The very practical book (make sure it's the current edition — it is updated annually) includes a fascinating workbook ("The Quick Job-Hunting Map").

Check out your local library or community college/university library for references on careers and career changing. The *College Blue Book* series may be very helpful in selecting colleges where degrees are offered. Also check out Peterson's Guides (...to Two-Year Colleges, ...to Four-Year Colleges, ...to Certificate Programs) for up-to-date information on institutions of higher education. The same libraries usually have excellent guides for preparing resumes and job interviewing techniques. The U.S. Department of Labor's *Occupational Outlook Handbook* (check your local library for the current year edition) has timely and succinct information of over 250 occupations and 107 million jobs: nature of the work, working conditions, employment information, training requirements, earning potential, and projections of industry growth or decline for the next ten years.

Make the Most of Job Changes

When you have new job or a change in the responsibilities of an old job, take advantage of the situation. Use the opportunity to organize yourself, ask for help, delegate whenever possible, verbalize your expectations, needs, limitations — to yourself, colleagues and superiors. Above all, accept your mistakes as learning opportunities, and always be patient with yourself.

Take Back Your Evenings

At the end of the working day, before you go home, write down the five most important things you have to do tomorrow. After doing this, number them in the order of their importance. At the beginning of the next day, start working on the most important thing! Some may find it more helpful to do this exercise first thing in the morning before beginning any other work.

Your evenings are a precious commodity. Be assertive with yourself and your job if you find yourself taking home work on a regular basis. Avoid any kind of activity that is even related to the job; create a pleasurable diversity.

Cut Work Pollution

Check out your working environment for uncomfortable, irritating noises, light levels, temperatures, vibrations, air pollutants (dirt, smoke, strong odors, chemical vapors). If any of these are creating pressure, creatively consider ways of changing the situation. Rearrange a desk, hang a picture, paint a wall, bring in a plant. Maybe you could even move your desk or office if you asked. Be resourceful. Even small changes will help. If changes are not possible, don't give up. Offset the negative conditions by engaging in some type of activity breaks, lunch periods, after work (exercise, sports, walk, hobbies, meditation).

Take Fun Breaks at Work

Even during the work day you can be in control and make the time more pleasurable. Create short periods of diversion (five minutes, fifteen minutes, thirty minutes, whatever). Here are some ideas: reading a favorite magazine or novel, listening to cassette tapes with music or motivational ideas, breathing/relaxing exercises, walking or meeting someone new at work during a break, wearing clothes that make you feel good, changing what you eat for lunch and where.

De-Stress Your Workplace

Share your ideas, hopes, and plans for distress reduction with your colleagues, but especially your supervisors. Encourage them to make distress awareness and reduction an organizational concern and priority. The statistics prove that less-distressed employees are more productive! Even minimal amounts of time off during the work day for distress-reducing activities pay big dividends.

Sit Down and Relax for Three Minutes!

What to do at work when you are becoming overwhelmed by the pressures? Here is a brief exercise which will help clear your mind and refresh a body that is tensing up. These techniques are not substitutes for a regular physical activity program, or for the more in-depth relaxation procedures described in Chapter 18. Nevertheless, this three-minute routine will help a lot when there is not time for anything more!

Begin this exercise sitting *straight* and toward the edge of a chair. *Smile* while you are enjoying the good feelings it produces!

1. *Breathe*: Take four-five slow, deep breaths and clear your mind of all concerns and thoughts.

2. *Neck & shoulders*: Raise your shoulders, trying to touch your ears with them. At the same time stretch out your arms in front of you. Tense your arms and shoulders and hold for five seconds. Then release....

Raise your shoulders again. This time stretch out your arms to the sides. Tense your arms and shoulders and hold for five seconds. Then release....Roll your head gently twice to the right and then twice to the left. Remember to keep breathing!

3. *Back*: Raise your arms above your head and pretend you are using your hands and arms to climb a ladder. Slowly and rhythmically continue for ten seconds. Then release....

While facing forward in your chair, *slowly* and *gently* turn your torso to the right as far as you can, trying if you can to grasp the back of the chair. Then turn to the left. Repeat this step again.

4. *Legs*: Lift your right leg. Roll your foot in a circle five times. Repeat for the left leg. Repeat the complete step again....Lift both legs. Bend your feet toward your head. Hold for five seconds. Then bend your feet away from your head. Hold for five seconds. Then release.

5. *Breathe*: Pick a pleasant and peaceful place to go to in your mind. Close your eyes. Release any tension you might feel anywhere in your body. For the next minute or so just breathe slowly and deeply.

6. *Reality*: Return to your activities refreshed and relieved. Use this three-minute mind and body break at the slightest hint of creeping tension.

Work Bibliography

Albrecht, *Stress and the Manager: Making It Work for You.*
Bolles, *What Color is Your Parachute?*
Charland, *Career Shifting: Starting Over in a Changing Economy*
Covey, *First Things First: To Live, To Learn, To Leave a Legacy*
Fanning, *Get It All Done and Still Be Human*
Freudenberger, *Burn Out: How to Beat the High Cost of Success*
Lakein, *How to Get Control of Your Time and Your Life*
Phelps and Austin, *The Assertive Woman: A New Look*
Walker, *Learn to Relax: 13 Ways to Reduce Tension*

For a more complete description of these books, please see "Suggested Readings," page 179.

15

Leisure Stress Buffers

"If you would not age, you must make everything you do touched with play, play of the body, play of the thought, of emotions. If you do, you will belong to that special class of people who find joy and happiness in every act, in every moment. Those to whom leisure is the one thing valuable."

— Dr. George Sheehan
Running and Being, the Total Experience

"You must first be convinced that leisure *is important, that you want more of it and are willing to change anything in life to get it."*

— Boenisch and Haney

*T*he short list of suggestions in this chapter will give you lots of ideas for immediate action you can take to combat your "leisure stress." None of the *stress buffers* is intended as a long-range answer to the leisure stress in your life, but every one of them offers a step you can take *now* — today, tomorrow, this week — toward reducing distress. Find two or three that fit your situation and try them out.

Leisure is not just sitting and relaxing, although sometimes it includes this activity. Leisure is discovering the playful child in you and giving it permission to laugh and frolic again. Leisure is anything that will *renew* your mind, body, and spirit!

Find Your Own Leisure

Sometimes people find it difficult to enjoy leisure activities because they don't know what they like (or have perhaps forgotten). Take a few leisurely minutes now and list your preferences. Do you like to play alone, with your age group, with both sexes? Do you like physical, intellectual, social, emotional or creative activities? What kind of feelings would you like from your leisure (achievement, recognition, relaxation, pleasure)? Do you want to spend your leisure time in town, in the country, by a lake, in a forest, on a beach? When do you like to be leisurely (morning, evening, on weekends, during holidays)? Pick the sports, games, activities, hobbies, crafts, or pastimes that match your preferences.

Schedule Leisure

Until you learn to be a leisurely person, on a regular basis, without feeling guilty — carefully schedule times to enjoy leisure. Think about leisure as you would think about a business trip, a doctor's appointment, a meal or any other scheduled commitment you would not miss.

Leisure for many people is enjoying friends. So many times, when we see or talk to special people, we tend to end our conversation with "Let's get together sometime." You know what usually happens: you never get together. Be assertive with yourself and those good friends. Take the extra few minutes to actually *arrange* something specific. People who do so rarely regret it.

Perhaps you are one of those many who procrastinate or feel guilty about leisure; *scheduled* leisure is a good way to begin. Consider classes and workshops in sports, games, wine-tasting, cooking, backpacking, dog obedience, fly tying, poetry appreciation, horseshoes, card games.... Local park and recreation offices and community colleges (ask for the "community services" program) usually provide exciting possibilities for very little expense.

Take One-Minute Vacations

Start small. Teach yourself *again* how to take thirty to sixty seconds to enjoy the small, fleeting beauties of life. When did you last pause long enough to really enjoy any of these...

- smell of a flower
- sight of clear, cool water
- a walk through leaves in the autumn
- a sunrise or sunset
- smell of burning wood
- smell of something baking
- warmth of the sun
- a cool breeze
- silence of the woods
- a rainbow
- freshly fallen snow

- a walk by a creek
- feel of leather
- feel of warm, moist lips
- a piece of art

- autumn leaves
- taste of popcorn
- birds singing

Take one minute now and add here any other experiences that make you feel more alive:

Many such experiences briefly enter each day. Look for them today, and take a one-minute vacation with them.

Visualize Small Escapes

Do you know what makes you happy? What relaxes you? Give yourself permission to escape mentally for brief moments into an unstructured world where you can relax and have fun. Some possibilities:

Mentally travel to:
- a deserted beach
- a log cabin
- a tree house
- the woods

- grandma's house
- a vacation spot of your dreams
- a warm, flowery meadow

Experience Small Escapes

Try:
- a warm bath
- wine or spring water, candlelight and incense in the bathroom
- a picnic on the living room floor with music
- a sauna
- reading a good book in bed
- sitting in front of a crackling fire with the lights out

- listening to a favorite album with earphones
- a slow shampoo from a loved one
- people watching
- window-shopping
- spending an entire evening surrounded only by candlelight
- bus riding for pleasure
- doing crossword or jigsaw puzzles
- bookstore browsing
- visiting craft shows and flea markets
- raising pets
- letter writing
- flying model airplanes or kites
- quilting
- wine-making
- flower-arranging
- watching educational TV

Choose Television Carefully

Make this invention a real source of relaxing entertainment and leisure. Preview the weekly schedule and decide in advance on several programs that you would enjoy alone or as a family or with friends. Turn on the television immediately before the scheduled program, and turn it off when the show is over. Stay away from violent or anxiety-producing topics. (You know what relaxes you or makes you uptight.) If the local or national news becomes depressing or overwhelming — turn it off. Try a weekly news magazine as a source of current events. Pick and choose what you read, watch, and hear!

Make Friends

Rekindle friendships. Send out invitations several weeks in advance for a potluck supper. Announce in your invitation the starting and ending time if this will keep it from becoming a hassle. Try potlucks with food themes. Try them in the neighborhood as a way of making new friends.

Reward Yourself

Tie your leisure to projects. Do a chore or task and have a specific leisure reward planned for yourself when you finish. Never deny yourself the reward. This works especially well with children. Try eating out once a week as a reward if everyone pitches in and cleans the house right after work, or Saturday, or *anytime*!

Make Space for Leisure

Create a specific area in the home for projects and hobbies. Even a section of a room is enough. Make it a quiet, relaxing place anyone in the home can use whenever he/she wants to think, unwind, create, or just be.

Try Biofeedback

Stress causes changes to occur continuously within your body, producing variations in your peripheral skin temperature, sweat gland activity, brain wave activity, heart rate, blood pressure and muscle contractions, to name a few. While these fluctuations are normally imperceptible, biofeedback instruments can amplify them, usually electronically, providing immediate information on the body-mind interaction. Biofeedback training is a way of quickly learning to control a wide variety of body functions that were once thought to be beyond conscious control. Relaxation, autogenic exercises and visualization are key ingredients used in conjunction with the actual biofeedback training. The benefit in learning to control any or all of these body functions is that you can *prevent* the occurrence or severity of many of the annoying results of stress: cold, clammy hands, tense neck, pounding heart, and others.

Dots?.... What's with The Dots?

Buy yourself a package of adhesive dots (any color that is pleasing and restful to you). Most office supply stores carry them. Place them in strategic locations in your environment. Some suggestions include the telephone, file cabinet, desk drawer, mirrors or dashboard of the car. The dots can serve as gentle reminders to practice breathing, relaxation, desk exercises, positive thinking or any other eustress skill.

Try Lunch-Time "Hideaways"

How do you spend your lunch time? Do you eat at the same place with the same people daily? Maybe you're cheating yourself. Those thirty or sixty minutes in the middle of your eight-hour day could be the most rewarding. This time offers you the opportunity for relaxation, fun and self-discovery. Try some of the following suggestions.

Health clubs. How about engaging in a physical fitness program during lunch? Talk to the people around you who are working out at lunch time and compare their complaints about tension, fatigue and headaches with the non-exercisers.

Museums. Try concentrating on one section at a time. Some of the larger museums even have cafeterias — you would not even have to miss lunch!

Television. Perhaps a lounge chair, feet up and your favorite soap opera could be another way of getting away from the tension at work. If going home is out of the question, bring a small black and white portable TV to work and share with those co- workers who enjoy the same show.

Beauty break. Treat your body to some luxury and get a haircut, shampoo, massage, sauna or facial session. Men as well as women are trying this one more and more.

Golf course. Nine holes is probably out of the question, but what about taking your frustrations out on a bucket of golf balls? You do not even have to know how to play golf to do this.

Flower shop, nursery. If you like plants, spend your time becoming more familiar with shrubs, trees and flowers. Being among plants away from the job is extremely restful.

Cemetery. To some a trip through the cemetery sounds morbid, but if you are interested in local history or researching genealogy, it can be fascinating.

Home decorating. Take as many lunch hours as necessary and browse through shops that carry paint, furniture and wallpaper. It takes time to get the rooms of your home or apartment the way you want, and it's easier when you are not under pressure to make immediate decisions. If you work fifty weeks a year, that gives you up to 250 lunch hours!

Class. Start a lunch time exercise class with other co-workers. Or find out some of their hobby areas and learn from one another.

Greeting card shop. Do you always dash in the last minute to buy that greeting card? It is much more pleasant to shop ahead of time. Put it on your calendar to buy cards once a month.

Public library. Try visiting the periodical section or the music section. Listening to a soothing selection with earphones while browsing through a favorite magazine is great for the mind and body.

Shopping or browsing in beautiful places such as art galleries, fine jewelry shops, antique stores or expensive boutiques has a very tranquil effect on many people. Stores of these types are very accustomed to having people "Just looking" and it costs nothing.

More... Lunch on a park bench, visit a travel agency or hobby store, take a walking tour of the city. Think up others. Try them. Consider them daily rewards.

Read Leisure Magazines

Subscribe to a leisure magazine. It could be any one of dozens that deal with a favorite pastime, hobby, craft, special interest, or activity that you currently enjoy or would like to try. For a few dollars a month or even less, the magazine will provide a few regular hours of fun. Any library can help you explore the wide range of magazines currently available.

Share Work and Leisure

Individuals and families sometimes complain about not having any time to relax because of "all the chores around the house." One family solved this problem by selecting a specific evening and time when they *all* shared the chores. They blocked out every Wednesday from 5:30 to 7:00. Every family member (mom, dad and the two children) had mutually agreeable duties which resulted in the most important chores getting done and ensured the work load was equalized. Tasks were rotated as much as possible. Everyone worked hard and afterwards all were rewarded with supper at a restaurant or a special TV show, or a rented movie, or a game played by the whole family. The immediate reward is very important. Their weekends, previously filled with work, are now scheduled for leisure activities.

Potpourri

Take a non-credit class or read books to relax or learn a new hobby. Trade skills with someone so you can learn from each other the new talent or hobby. Buy season tickets for something you enjoy (you are then *committed* to attend). Take twenty minutes at the beginning of every month and actually schedule on a calendar something leisurely to do *every* week (as a minimum).

Leisure Bibliography

Benson and Klipper, *The Relaxation Response*

Buxbaum, *Sports for Life: Fitness Training, Injury Prevention and Nutrition*

Downing, *The Massage Book*

Fast, *The Pleasure Book*

Hendricks, and Willis, *The Centering Book: Awareness Activities for Children, Parents and Teachers*

Johnson, *838 Ways to Amuse a Child*

LeShan, *How to Meditate*

Ryan and Travis, *Wellness Workbook*

Stein, *Family Games*

Walker, *Learn to Relax*

Watterson, *The Authoritative Calvin and Hobbes* (one of eight books and treasuries to date of the cartoon characters, Calvin and Hobbes)

Weinstein and Goodman, *Playfair: Everybody's Guide to Non-Competitive Play*

For a more complete description of these books, please see "Suggested Readings," page 179.

16

Mind Stress Buffers

*T*he short list of suggestions in this chapter will give you lots of ideas for immediate action you can take to combat your "mind stress." None of the *stress buffers* is intended as a long-range answer to the mind stress in your life, but every one of them offers a step you can take *now* — today, tomorrow, this week — toward reducing distress. Find two or three that fit your situation and try them out.

Find Meaning and Fulfillment

Why am I here? What is the purpose of my existence? Is there a life force or power that is present in my life and in the world? What is the truth? How do I find the sacred? Is there a God? If so, how do I develop a personal, meaningful, fulfilling relationship?

For many the answer to more meaning, more fulfillment, being loved, feeling important, is found in a special, close relationship with their God — Supreme Being, higher consciousness, Buddha, universal life force, or other personal concept of a spirit which transcends human experience. But, how do you go about developing such a relationship, especially one that touches your inner being and creates an undeniable sense of being loved?

There are several techniques we will share with you which can be the avenue to creating an inner life and strength. However, we also want to share a warning. *Finding more meaning and fulfillment often does not happen quickly*. That may be hard for some of you living in our fast-paced society to accept.

The techniques which work for people are based on mental (inner) quiet and reflection as well as physical relaxation and rhythmic breathing. Your body and mind are focused and open.

• Some find their way to God through *books*. A few which have helped others in "opening the door" are listed at the end of this chapter.

• Others find their personal God through *reflection on sacred texts*. Among the books that may assist you in this refreshing and insightful process include: *The Bible* (Christianity), *The Torah* (Judaism), *Tao Te Ching* (Taoism), *Dharma* (Buddhism), *Qur'an* (Islam), and *The Vedas* (Hinduism) depending on your religious preference. The wisdom and spirituality shared by individuals over the centuries have a number of common "threads" woven through them. The similarity of the messages can provide hope and strength to those who search them out.

• *Meditation or contemplation,* the mentally quiet and physically relaxing time when we can allow ourselves "to be," is another popular and proven way to walk the path of deeper meaning and fulfillment. Personal prayer complements meditation (before, during or after) and can be a powerful source of insight and comfort. Helpful books include: *Prayer: Finding the Heart's True Home,* and *How to Meditate*.

• Some people experience their God when they become a part of a *community*. Different religious groups have their own unique approaches and atmospheres. Many people find the most supportive and compatible group by actually visiting them for a service or two before making a commitment. Others find a deep sense of peace and a connection with a higher presence by being in the wonders and beauty of nature. It may not be the fact that you frequent a church building or go to a beautiful outside location that brings you closer to the divine, sacred and mystical. It may be that these locations allow you to escape the hectic pace of your life and allow you to quiet your mind so that the sacred has an opportunity to manifest itself without competition and distractions. It seems curious that so many prison inmates find "religion" until you realize how much time they have to contemplate and be alone with themselves and the sacred presence that may be closer than we realize.

• Another way of meeting your God is through *friends*. Ask them about their faith and beliefs. Find out how they came to experience the joys of a loving God. Most people won't push their beliefs or religion and are usually very sincere about sharing when asked.

• If it is important to give yourself time and quiet in order to find the sacred, we would suggest that it is just as important to be at peace with yourself and others and with the everyday activities in your world.

We urge you to begin first by accepting and truly loving who you are: *finding inner peace with yourself.* Then work on being at peace with others, letting go of resentments, expectations, judgments and demands. Finally, find simple joy, relaxation and inner peace in the everyday activities of your life. Inner tranquility in the midst of the world and in the midst of others is your goal. You will find your God, higher power, the source of meaning, the sacred and mystical by recognizing its presence within yourself, in others, in your world and in your every moment.

The secret is that we are in daily, constant contact with the goal of our personal, spiritual quest but we don't have the ears, eyes, and mind to recognize it. Be patient, give yourself quiet time and you may discover what you yearn to behold.

Get Satisfied with Yourself

The "bad" news: as hard as it may be to accept, you allowed yourself to be who you are now. The good news: what you created you can uncreate; you can change yourself to be who you want to be.

• Identify *specifically and realistically*, in writing, what you would like to change.

• Decide how you can use the strengths you already have or develop different ones.

• Look around at friends or acquaintances who have strengths you would like to acquire. Ask them how they developed them.

• Ask those close to you what they see in you: both the strengths as well as the "rough edges." Ask them for insight as to how you can grow and then ask them for support in the process.

Meditate

Giving your mind a rest period is important. Meditation comes in many forms. Some, like Transcendental Meditation, involve money and classes to learn. Other forms can be very simple, yet just as effective depending on how serious you are. A good book to begin with is *How to Meditate* by Lawrence LeShan.

Seek Peaks

Analyze those times you have considered "peak experiences" (those times which have made you feel "high" and positive about yourself and life itself). Then plan for them to happen by including the same people, events or places in your life at regular intervals. Wanting special experiences to happen can create them. One place to start is the checklist in the Leisure chapter, "Take One-Minute Vactions" and "Visualize Small Escapes."

Find Solitude

Being alone with yourself and not experiencing loneliness is a great gift. You can practice being in solitude. When you are ready, set aside several hours and be in a special, quiet place to think, pray, meditate, write in a journal, experience feelings — by yourself, for yourself. A great book is Anthony Storr's *Solitude: A Return to the Self*. You can find more meaning, more fulfillment and more health not by searching outwardly, but by going inside yourself. There you will find yourself, your source of strength, Life itself.

Practice Relaxation

Almost every self-help or stress book mentions this very important way of revitalizing your physical and intellectual energies. Some provide extensive written instructions for systematically relaxing (see Chapter 18). Advertisements for cassette tapes appear in more and more popular magazines. Almost anyone with a calm, soothing voice, however, could record instructions onto tape for personal use. Some respond especially well to their own voice on tape. This technique can be used almost anywhere, in any amount of time available from thirty seconds to thirty minutes. This simple remedy is free and, if it is used consistently and conscientiously, can be one of the most effective means of combating distress.

Give Up Television

Sell the TV if it is interfering with your life! Or at least move the set to an out-of-the-way room. Let TV be a source of intellectual stimulation, not a millstone that pulls you down into mindless oblivion. See Chapter 15 for more ideas.

Read

• Visit your local college and/or public library.

• Set a goal to read one book a week, or one a month, or some comfortable number; then *do* it!

• Make time to read. The time can be short (ten minutes) or long periods. Let reading become a habit. Some like to spend time reading in bed as a way to unwind, relax and fall to sleep.

• Ask your friends for recommendations of good books that are in line with your tastes.

• Don't forget magazines. But be selective; don't have eight to ten magazines arriving every week unless you can realistically read them. Make reading relaxing, not a chore.

• Read for personal growth. For example, review the books sold by our publisher, Impact Publishers. Many are listed in our list of suggested readings. Impact even has a toll free number for orders: 1-800-2-IMPACT or check with your local bookstore.

Change Your Thoughts

You are in control of what you think. If you find yourself being plagued by negative, distressful, depressing thoughts, stop for five to ten seconds and mentally tell the unwanted thoughts to "STOP." Then, immediately start creating positive images of relaxation, tranquility, and pleasant relationships with others.

Travel

• Draw a 50 or100 mile radius around your home and plan one-day trips to places you have never been.

• Find out about the lower travel costs offered by travel groups and on airlines offering "super-savers."

• Change your own perspective on what is or can be relaxing! You don't have to go to Las Vegas to enjoy the sun.

• Try camping instead of "motelling" it.

Discuss

Organize a discussion group of friends to meet periodically and discuss current issues, books, travel, hobbies, plays, music, local history, recreation, politics, religion, even ways to deal with distress!

Practice Yoga

Learn to relax utilizing this Far Eastern method of cultivating good health. It can give you a new vital source of energy, help in quieting the mind, and a new way to handle distress.

Regain Control

Many people continually accept more and more positions, tasks, or jobs. Overload results: feelings of being overwhelmed, pressured, unable to do justice to anything, illness, depression, the list goes on. There are no superwomen or supermen, only women and men who cling to the belief that they can do it all, only they can do it right, no one else cares, and on and on. It is not a sign of weakness to accept the fact that you have limited time and energy. Rather, it is a sign of unrealistic, presumptuous thinking to continue to act like God. If you're overwhelmed now, carefully evaluate each obligation and make some choices about what has to go. Be careful about taking on new responsibilities without carefully evaluating the ramifications to your health, to your career, to your relationships.

Get Organized

Get more done in less time. Organization is a matter of habit. Analyze what is wasting your time and why. Begin by prioritizing things, organizing your work environment, preventing interruptions, and delegating responsibilities. See Chapter 21 for some other ideas in this area.

Seek New Avenues

• Explore some new sources of intellectual development.
• Enroll in a college course covering a special subject you've been wanting to know about.
• Forget the distress of exams by signing up for "audit" (enrolling for informational purposes only, not for credit).
• Try a new hobby.
• Invite a friend to join you in developing new insights and interests. Be creative and adventurous.

Mind Bibliography

Alberti and Emmons, *Your Perfect Right: A Guide to Assertive Living*
Benson, *The Relaxation Response*
Bible
Brown, *Stress and the Art of Biofeedback*
Cousins, *Head First: The Biology of Hope*
Cousins, *The Healing Heart: Antidotes to Panic and Helplessness*
Covey, *The 7 Habits of Highly Effective People*
Dossey, *Healing Words: The Power of Prayer and The Practice of Medicine*
Fanning, *Get It All Done and Still Be Human*
Foster, *Prayer: Finding the Heart's True Home*
Gaedwag, (Ed.), *Inner Balance: The Power of Holistic Healing*
Gendlin, *Focusing*
Gibran, *The Prophet*
Goldberg and Kaufman, *Natural Sleep: How to Get Your Share*
Kushner, *When Bad Things Happen to Good People*

Lakein, *How to Get Control of Your Time and Your Life*

Lazarus, *Don't Believe it for a Minute!: Forty Toxic Ideas that are Driving You Crazy*

LeShan, *How to Meditate: A Guide to Self-Discovery*

Mandino, *The Greatest Miracle in the World*

Mantell, *Don't Sweat the Small Stuff: (P.S. It's ALL Small Stuff!)*

McKay and Dinkmeyer, *How You Feel is Up to You: The Power of Emotional Choice*

Millman, *Secret of the Peaceful Warrior*

Moyers, *Healing and the Mind*

Novak, *The World's Wisdom: Sacred Texts of the World's Religions*

Peale, *The Power of Positive Thinking*

Peck, *The Road Less Traveled*

Pelletier, *Mind as Healer, Mind as Slayer*

Phelps and Austin, *The Assertive Woman: A New Look*

Preston, *Growing Beyond Emotional Pain: Action Plans for Healing*

Preston, *You Can Beat Depression: A Guide to Prevention and Recovery*

Robbins, *Unlimited Power*

Siegel, *Love, Medicine and Miracles*

Simonton, Matthew-Simonton and Creighton, *Getting Well Again*

Storr, *Solitude: A Return to the Self*

Walker, *Learn to Relax*

Watterson, *The Authoritative Calvin and Hobbes* (one of eight books and treasuries to date of the cartoon characters, Calvin and Hobbes)

Young and Jones, *Sidetracked Home Executives*

For a more complete description of these books, please see "Suggested Readings," page 179.

17

Body Stress Buffers

*T*he short list of suggestions in this chapter will give you lots of ideas for immediate action you can take to combat your "body stress." None of the *stress buffers* is intended as a long-range answer to the body stress in your life, but every one of them offers a step you can take *now* — today, tomorrow, this week — toward reducing distress. Find two or three that fit your situation and try them out.

Decompress
   Sound like a *scuba* diving technique to avoid physical distress? Actually, it is a type of time management technique which helps you keep the distress in one area of your life from spilling over into and contaminating other areas.
   It's a classic story: Carolyn was so angered at work that she ran people off the road on the way home, slammed the door on the way into the house, screamed at the innocent and bewildered children, and kicked the dog (a great example of raw, inexcusable aggression).
   We all need to be able to let down in a healthy, controlled way and thus "decompress" after one activity before going on to the next. It is especially important to decompress between work and home, but you should also do it between demanding activities throughout the day so you can be your most efficient, effective, and lovable self.
   What will work? *Almost anything!* Look inside yourself at your needs. What helps you unwind? What helps you put something out of your mind? Use it as long as it is healthy for yourself and others.

Some other basic principles about decompression to keep in mind:
- you need to want to do it
- be specific about when and what you are going to do
- have several options in case one does not feel right
- vary the activity or technique from time to time
- know how much time it will take
- don't work so hard at decompressing that you become distressed trying
- adopt an attitude that says you deserve the time to rejuvenate yourself.

The time you take for yourself will provide you with more energy, more enthusiasm, and more productivity. Test it out, then believe and enjoy!

Over the years, we have assembled a collection of decompression techniques. A word of caution: be open-minded about the techniques. Many may need to be modified to fit your lifestyle:

- Watch the evening news, read the newspaper or a magazine (for some, this in itself will cause more distress)
- Open the mail (could also be distressful at times!)
- Clean a room or a portion of a room
- Take a fifteen to twenty minute nap
- Engage in physical activity
- Share the ups and downs of the day, up to maximum of fifteen to twenty minutes, with your spouse, children, a friend, a pet
- Meditate or relax for a few quality minutes
- Pray while you are driving home (don't close your eyes), as you fix supper, while you are relaxing, or almost anytime
- Take a few minutes to mentally review the day; look forward to the evening or tomorrow, organize yourself for the next day, make a list of things to do
- Get out of the house or into a quieter part of the house if possible, with the help of your spouse or friend, to do something special by yourself and for yourself
- Have a cup or glass of your favorite non-alcoholic, non-caffeine drink
- Take a quick or leisurely shower or bath (alone or with someone)
- Take a leisurely or brisk walk after supper

You have the idea. Almost anything will work. The worst thing you can do is to say you "don't have the time" to decompress. A man in one of our seminars told us how he would mentally hang each of his cares and worries as leaves on a big tree he passed on his way home from work. And, given that the wind blows so much in Wyoming, the leaves (cares and worries) were never there the next day.

You need to be good to yourself. You deserve it! If you don't do something to decompress and make a smooth transition from distressful situations, you will not be able to keep up the pace, physically or psychologically.

Volunteer

There is a phenomenon where individuals that do good, feel good. It has been noted that those individuals who volunteer in their communities feel better and have additional energy. Just think of it, your needs and someone else's can both be met at the same time.

Shadow Box

If you need something new and different, try boxing. Box aerobics is a total body workout which involves actual shadow boxing including a jabs, punches and spins.

Eat Better

Continue to pay attention to your nutrition. A little thing like switching from whole milk to skim can help lower your cholesterol level. Read up on nutrition. Some communities have classes or even nutrition counseling available. Even local newspapers seem to be printing regular features about various aspects of healthy eating. Study your eating habits and decide what you need to change, if anything, to create the best balance. If you need to lose a small or large amount of weight, do not go on a crash diet. Adopt a long-term program of readjusting your eating habits to keep the joy in eating while taking in fewer calories. If you are extremely overweight, have a medical exam and get your doctor's advice. Books on this subject are many and varied. We've listed a few later in the chapter. Also, Chapter 19 expands on this topic.

Join a Support Group

Almost every community offers support groups through county extension offices, colleges, school districts, YMCA's, YWCA's, mental health centers, or private organizations. Such groups are often free and exist for exercising, nutrition, dieting, smoking, relaxation. Dealing with any of these areas is much easier if it is done with others.

Exercise

The first step in doing something for your body is to *decide* to do it. Do not increase your exercise or start a program without making sure you are in reasonably good health. If you are over thirty-five or have any history of physical problems, have a medical examination and a physician's approval and advice on a good exercise program. It would help to choose a doctor who is physically fit and a regular exerciser! Give exercise a high priority in your life. Take your time, develop good habits, and most important of all, make exercise a pleasant growth experience. A wealth of books is available. Browse through any library or bookstore for titles listed at the end of this chapter. More on exercise in Chapter 20.

Stop Smoking

Give it up, *completely*! Do anything: read, visit professionals, talk to people — anything that will move you to break your drug addiction. Physical exercise will many times help greatly in stopping. Talk to the American Cancer Society or the Lung Association — they have free literature.

Watch Your Drinking

You may feel you should change your alcohol habits. Start slowly. Find other sources of relaxation: exercise, sports, friends who will be supportive, reading, relaxation exercises, meditation, music, anything that will be right for you. Cut back with the help of local organizations (their services are usually free).

Cut Back on Drugs

We refer not to the "hard" drugs so much as to those everyday recreational drugs that have made their way into your life — tranquilizers, caffeine, nicotine, or any medicine to which you can develop a habit. Coffee, tea and soft drinks all contain habit-forming caffeine. Taper off gradually. You do not have to give up caffeine completely, but reduce your intake to a level that will not add to your stress reaction.

Find a Quiet Place

If you do not have a special place in your home that can be a quiet, personal, and private retreat — be good to yourself and create one *today*! If you live with others, let them know about your quiet place so they can respect your privacy and needs when you are there. Invite them to use your retreat or to create their own. Children can benefit from this just as much as adults. Help them early in life to find the value and strength in being in a personal, restful place all their own. If physical space is not available, you can develop a "quiet corner" and encourage others to respect your needs.

Improve Your Sex Life

Sometimes sex therapy is needed to resolve some difficulties. Usually, a trusting, honest attitude and good communication go a long way. Some books can be excellent guides to deeper fulfillment and adventure: *Joy of Sex; The Massage Book; Our Bodies, Ourselves.*

Discover Holistic Health

Throughout this book we have emphasized the importance of concern for mind, body, spirit and relationships. Some excellent books are available to help you understand and appreciate the fulfillment that can result from the integration of your mind, spirit, and body into a holistic unity. *High Level Wellness* is one of the best. It contains an extensive annotated bibliography for further reading

Care for Aching Feet

Remember that keeping your feet in shape will make the difference in your fitness program. If you are female, every time you slip on a pair of high heels you put seventy-six percent more weight on the balls of your feet. There are tremendous benefits of daily foot routine. You are dependent on your feet to keep you active and on-the-move. Plus, it is difficult to put that best foot forward if it's killing you. During the course of your life it is estimated that you will walk the equivalent of four times around the world. That is quite a difference in the wrong pair of shoes. If your feet hurt, then they are trying to tell you something. It could be a comment on the shoes you have purchased.

Check for Osteoporosis

It used to be that a woman would not be aware that she had a problem with osteoporosis until symptoms appeared. Many clinics now have bone densitometers, a new type of x-ray that measures the density of bones. The test has proved to be fast and accurate. Check it out! Once you have gotten the reading from the test, ask your doctor about medication, nutrition and other forms of prevention.

Learn While You Burn

Exercise bikes and similar machines are often abandoned because the workout is boring. Here's a tip that may keep you going: You can now buy from the Sierra Club a computer screen saver that shows full-color pictures of nature. What a way to entertain yourself when you are on that stationary bike as well as saving your computer. Other possibilities for mental exercise to accompany physical include listening to audiotapes, watching videotapes, and book stands that mount on your handlebars.

Get an Aromatic High

The right perfume can give you a psychological lift but it might also improve your jogging or tennis game. If a fragrance smells like a cooling flavor (menthol for instance), then by sniffing a bit your energy will lift a bit. Remember too the quieting effect some fragrances like lavender have in the bathtub. Floral fragrances have even been tried in dentists' offices in order to reduce anxiety. And believe it or not, it works!

Be aware that some individuals are allergic to various scents like perfumes, colognes, diesel, gasoline, hair sprays. If you are having unusual reactions like headaches, lightheadedness, "fuzzy thinking," you might want to have yourself checked for allergies.

Go for a Mental Jog

You need to exercise your mind as well as your body. Mental stimulation has been found to ward off diseases like dementia. Plus if you can continue to keep your mind thinking, aging is certainly delayed.

Find Your Rhythm

No matter what kind of exercise you find, develop a rhythm. Even if the only time you have during the day for exercise is at your desk, you can take a mini-vacation by allowing all distractions to float away and by keeping your mind focused on the movements of your feet. While you run, pay attention only to your footsteps; as you swim, concentrate on the sound of your strokes. It certainly will pay off.

Hug a Tree

There is a new field of psychology called eco-psychology. Eco-psychologists recommend that when life is getting you down, the best therapy is a walk in the woods and the development of a relationship with a tree.

Relax

When was the last time you went kite-flying, flower-picking, or just walking to take in the scenery? Relaxation in a beautiful environment provides tremendous benefits for both your body and mind. As is the case with any activity, endorphins are released and the kite and your spirits soar!

Get Sleep

Everything you feel, hear or visualize can influence your sleep. A total body massage can put you into "seventh heaven" or if that is not possible from another, try giving yourself a foot massage. You probably would do well to avoid violent or disturbing television after altogether. Also, your bedroom should be a pleasant environment to curl up in (you wonder how your teenager ever gets to sleep).

Views from windows, fish tanks, fireplaces, a favorite painting, can have a stress-relieving effect. Keeping your bed made and your room clean can create that extra harmony that you need. Turn a space into a mini gallery of objects that have special meaning. They can be a connection to the past or just more recent memories. Just like violent t.v. shows, loud or heavy music can also create the negative. Try music that emulates your biological rhythms. Try out some new age or classical, or whatever is soothing to you.

Common sense says that you probably need to avoid caffeine, nicotine or alcohol. A late night dinner might be the European style, but eating a huge meal at night could keep you going, and going, and going. Your grandmother's suggestion of warm milk could be just the trick you need. Warm foods are more relaxing than cold foods. Sweet fragrances can also create a mood of relaxation. A room can smell tense or calm, so use aromas that have a balancing effect on your mood.

Try Feng Shui

There is a Chinese practice that is known as Feng Shui. It is the belief of improving your life by controlling what is in your environment. It began as Taoist theory but can be applied to your life as you deal with day-to-day chaos. The Chinese recommend a variety of cures such as wind chimes and goldfish bowls in order to bring harmony into a room and into your life. According to this theory, your desk should be placed in order to have the clearest view of the door, thus avoiding surprise intrusions. Hang a green plant above the toilet to avoid flushing away good luck. Don't keep anything around, like old dried flowers, that have lost their life and beauty. Keep live flowers or pictures of flowers to symbolize life. Wind chimes as they ring are supposed to lift your spirits.

Give Yourself Credit when You Deserve It.

That includes credit for handling the major roles in your life: parenthood, breadwinner, cook and bottle washer.

Break Your Repetitive Motion Habits

If your job requires that you maintain one position for hours — e.g., sitting at a computer with your fingers on a keyboard — you may experience stiffness in certain muscle groups and/or joints. Medical researchers have identified a specific condition — *repetitive motion syndrome* — that commonly results from working at a job that involves hours of repeating the same pattern of motion. Frequent problem areas are knees, lower back, hands and wrists, elbows, neck and shoulders. If your job, or some other aspect of your life (e.g., exercise, a hobby...) places you in such a situation, *take regular breaks!* Don't keep at it until you're sore! (Computer users, for example, are advised to take several minutes away from the screen and keyboard each hour.) Get up and walk around. Practice a relaxation or meditation exercise with your eyes closed. (Tell your boss in advance what you're up to!)

Boost Your Ego

Carry a 3X5 card with all your good points or the great things you do. When your ego needs a little boosting, pull out the card and read...

Choose Happiness

You choose whether or not to be happy every day. After enough days of making the right choice, being happy will become a habit.

Think You Can

Once you have decided to take on something new, how do you overcome the jitters? Try immersing yourself in the activity by reading about it, watching videos about it, practicing it. Visualize yourself being successful. Feel alive and happy.

Act the Age You Want To Be

Age is a matter of the mind in many ways. It is also true that you can think yourself young. In our American society, we tend to grow older when society determines that we are old. Who says you have to be old at thirty, forty, fifty or sixty-five? Do you suddenly get up one day and say, "Gee, it's my birthday and today I am too old to do this"? Of course not. Find out what is important to you and what makes your heart want to beat. Then set about making these things a bigger part of your life.

Body Bibliography

Ardell, *High Level Wellness: An Alternative to Doctors, Drugs, and Disease*

Boston Women's Health Collective, *Our Bodies, Ourselves: A Book by and for Women*

Brody, *Jane Brody's Nutrition Book*

Chopra, *Ageless Body, Timeless Mind: The Quantum Alternative to Growing Old*

Chopra, *Restful Sleep: The Complete Mind-Body Program for Overcoming Insomnia*

Comfort, *The Joy of Sex*

Downing, *The Massage Book*

Hastings, Fadiman and Gordon (eds.), *Health for the Whole Person: The Complete Guide to Holistic Medicine*

Rossbach, *Interior Design with Feng Shui*

Selye, *Stress Without Distress*

University of California at Berkeley, *University of California at Berkeley Wellness Letter: The Newsletter of Nutrition, Fitness, and Stress Management*

Wilen, *Live and Be Well*

For a more complete description of these books, please see
"Suggested Readings," page 179.

18

Stress Relief: Relaxation

*T*ry this simple test. Place one hand on your chest and the other hand on your stomach. Breathe normally for thirty seconds. If the hand on your chest is moving, you are like most people who are not using the simplest yet most effective stress management technique available.

Breathing affects your whole body. When you are angry your breathing probably becomes irregular. Fear or stress usually produces quick and shallow breaths. A relaxed state is characterized by breathing that is slow, deep and regular. When you take a few seconds to breathe slowly, deeply and regularly in a stressful situation, you produce a state of relaxation.

Correct breathing actually short-circuits the stress response and promotes relaxation. In addition, correct breathing can strengthen and condition the pulmonary system, building up a respiratory reserve and increasing the capacity of the blood to carry oxygen throughout the body. The whole cardiovascular system can be enhanced, and nerves calmed, by using breathing techniques.

The key to correct breathing is to allow your diaphragm to do what it was designed to do. This simple muscle, located beneath your ribs, is supposed to expand *downward* when you inhale. This means your stomach should move out gently. In normal breathing, your rib cage can move outward — but not a lot. Most people try to keep their stomachs pulled in and breathe by raising their rib cages each time they inhale. This is awkward and takes a lot of energy, continually lifting a heavy rib cage when it was not designed to move so much in normal breathing. Exhaling should be a very gentle, effortless process: your diaphragm is relaxed and it pushes the air out as your stomach comes in.

Try the test again. This time as you hold your hand on your stomach, try lifting your hand by gently pushing out your stomach. You will be inhaling effortlessly as you do this. Breathe slowly for several minutes to become accustomed to the feeling.

In *any* stressful situation, no matter where you are, you can consciously use a simple breathing technique to reduce the tension and produce some relaxation. This technique, which takes only thirty-five to forty seconds, consists of the following steps:

1. Stand or sit as erect as possible and try to take your mind off of the stressful situation or activities around you.
2. Take a slow, deep breath while counting to three.
3. Hold your breath gently for a count of three.
4. Exhale slowly for a count of three.
5. Pause for a count of three.
6. Repeat this sequence three times.
7. Return to your activities.

How Do You Spell "Relaxation"?

Recently, when asked how they relaxed, people responded in a variety of ways:

"Let me watch a good football game and I'll relax."

"I take an aspirin and go to bed."

"For me, it's a scotch-on-the-rocks while watching the evening news."

"A favorite rock album through headphones while studying is relaxation for me."

"When I need to relax, I run a hot bath and soak for five minutes."

Unfortunately, not one of these individuals is relaxing well enough to significantly reduce tension and stress! At best, they are engaged in a favorite pastime that might be fun and satisfying.

The relaxation response is a physical and mental technique that counteracts the stress response, creating a return to normal. Balance is achieved within the system. Complete relaxation involves learning to recognize and feel tension in every muscle of the body, and how to release it.

Four basic elements are required to learn the relaxation response:

1. *A quiet place to practice.* Pick a time and a place where you are unlikely to be interrupted for twenty to thirty minutes. It helps to use the same location, at the same time, and to tell the children, spouse, friends what you will be doing. This special place should be as quiet and comfortable as possible. Dim the lights and loosen any tight clothing before practicing. You should also avoid practicing immediately before retiring (you will probably fall asleep and won't learn the techniques) or after a meal (your body is too busy with digestion to concentrate on muscle relaxation).

2. *A comfortable position.* Use a favorite chair or sofa which supports your body evenly. Avoid lying down on the floor or a bed, or taking another position in which you are likely to fall asleep. Your head should be supported, however, so you can relax your neck.

3. *A phrase or word to help you concentrate* may be helpful as you learn the technique of relaxing. Some suggestions include:

PHRASES	WORDS
I am relaxing	Relax
I feel peaceful	Peace
My mind is quiet	Quiet
I am calm	Calm
I feel healing and energy	Healing
I am being renewed	Renew

After you have mastered the skill of relaxing, your word or phrase will be your key to activating the relaxation response. Anytime, anywhere, you can mentally say this word or phrase and your mind will work with your body to produce a relaxed state in five to ten minutes. That's your goal.

4. *A passive attitude* is the last element needed to learn the relaxation response. Follow the "relaxation instructions" and *allow* the relaxation to develop. Allow the tension to flow out of your body, effortlessly. Do not try to force yourself or work too hard. Just let it happen.

Deep Muscle Relaxation

Deep relaxation is one of the most effective yet simplest techniques you can employ to reduce the effects of stress. It is also free and can be learned on your own in less than two weeks, practicing fifteen to thirty minutes a day.

The instructions provided on the next pages can be memorized, tape recorded by you or someone with a soothing voice, or read aloud by a friend.

After the instructions are completed, remain in this relaxed state for as long as you wish. If any tension creeps in, simply let it go as soon as you notice it. When you want to continue with your other activities, slowly open your eyes and continue to sit quietly for fifteen to thirty seconds. Then slowly move and resume activity. You should feel refreshed, awake and calm.

After using the instructions or tape five to seven times, try relaxing without them. You will find that you can *mentally* progress through the process in less and less time. You should also be able to begin relaxing completely, without going through the tensing stage, by simply focusing on a muscle group and allowing it to relax. At the same time, allow the relaxation in one area to flow into another area. Eventually you should be able to use your relaxation skills at any time and place, without interrupting your activities, by simply repeating your relaxation word or phrase several times when you notice muscle tension. Once activated, your relaxation response will take over and produce a relaxed state for you in just a few minutes.

Relaxation Technique: *Mental Relaxation Place* (Five to ten minutes)*

1. Select a comfortable sitting or reclining position.

2. Close your eyes, and think about a place that you have been before that represents your ideal place for physical and mental relaxation. (It should be a quiet environment, perhaps the seashore, the mountains, or even your own back yard. If you can't think of an ideal relaxation place, then create one in your mind.)

3. Now imagine that you are actually in your ideal relaxation place. Imaging that you are seeing all the colors, hearing the sounds, smelling the aromas. Just lie back, and enjoy your soothing, rejuvenating environment.

4. Feel the peacefulness, the calmness, and imagine your whole body and mind being renewed and refreshed.

5. After five to ten minutes, slowly open your eyes and stretch. You have the realization that you may instantly return to your relaxation place whenever you desire, and experience a peacefulness and calmness in body and mind.

Relaxation Technique: *Thinking About Muscle Groups* (Twenty minutes)*

1. Select a comfortable place to lie down. Remove shoes, loosen belt or light clothing. Stretch out on your back, arms resting by your sides, feet slightly apart, eyes gently closed.

2. Think to yourself, "I am now going to relax completely. When I awaken I will feel fully refreshed."

3. Think about your feet, wiggle your toes, flex your ankles. Then "let go" — let go of all the tension, and let your feet rest limp and heavy.

4. Think of the lower part of your legs, your knees and thighs, up to your hips. Imagine them just sinking into the floor, heavy and relaxed.

5. Now think of your hands. Wiggle your fingers and flex your wrists, then let go, relax.

6. Think of your lower arm, elbow, and upper arm, all the way up to your shoulders. Picture all the tension just melting away.

7. Think about your abdomen. Let the tension go, and allow your breathing to flow more smoothly and deeply.

8. Think about your stomach and chest, up to your throat and neck. As you continue breathing more deeply, just imagine all the tension flowing out and you are relaxing more and more.

9. Now think about your throat, neck, and head, feeling limp and relaxed. Relax your facial muscles. Drop the jaw, parting the lips and teeth. Picture yourself completely relaxed.

10. If you are aware of any remaining tension anywhere in the body, go to the area mentally and relax the tension.

11. Continue to remain in this completely relaxed state for five to ten minutes. You may picture pleasant thoughts, or simply blank your mind and enter a stage of light sleep.

12. When you are ready to awaken, say to yourself, "I have been deeply relaxed. I am now ready to wake up, feeling completely refreshed and relaxed."

13. Begin to wake up by flexing the ankles, wiggling the toes. Then wiggle the fingers, and gently shake your wrists.

14. Bend the right knee, and then the left knee. Bend the right arm, then the left arm.

15. Open your eyes. Stretch each arm over your head. Then slowly sit up, stand up, and stretch again. You are ready to continue with your activities.

---

*Developed by Dr. Cary Howard McCarthy. From *Stress and the Art of Biofeedback* by Barbara B. Brown. © 1977 by Barbara B. Brown. Used by permission of Bantam Books, Inc. All rights reserved.

Three-Minute Relaxing Exercise

Often it is necessary to find the most expedient means to relax during high stress situations. The following is an example of a *short* relaxation exercise that is beneficial on a daily basis. This exercise is not to take the place of deep muscle relaxation but can be used in addition, to provide some feelings of general relaxation and to prevent headaches or other physical symptoms. This exercise can be used anywhere or any time you have three minutes (A good use of transition time between activities, appointments or projects! Great for traffic jams or commuter trains, too!):

1. *Interrupt your thoughts.* Stop thinking about your surroundings and switch your thoughts to your breathing. Take two deep breaths from your abdomen and exhale slowly. As you are exhaling, say to yourself: "I am becoming very relaxed."

2. *Scan your body for tense or uncomfortable areas.*

    a) With the power of your mind's eye, look for any tension in your calves, thighs and buttocks. Release any tension you find.

    b) Now, use your mind's eye to search out any tension in your stomach, chest and back. Simply let any tension you find flow gently out of your body with the next breath.

    c) Again, with the power of your mind's eye, try to detect any tension that may be in your shoulders, neck, jaws, eyes or forehead. Let any tension melt away as warm ripples of relaxation flow from the top of your head to your feet.

3. *Concentrate for fifteen seconds on warming your hands.* Feel the warm waves of relaxation flowing freely to your fingertips, making them warmer and warmer.

4. *Pick a pleasant thought, image, memory or feeling.* Remain with it for a few seconds.

5. *Take another deep breath and return to your activities.*

Leisuring Your Way to Less Stress

Almost without exception, books, articles and experts in stress management place heavy emphasis on breathing and relaxation as two of the most effective avenues for reducing stress. The explanation for the beneficial effects of these techniques lies in the body-mind connection. Your body functions and well-being are directly influenced by what you do with your mind. Helping and then allowing your mind to become calm, uncluttered, peaceful, and passive will have a beneficial effect on your body and your lifestyle. Try the suggestions for breathing and relaxation in this chapter. You may be surprised at this new dimension of leisure!

Relaxation Music

Relaxation music is available, usually through local record, cassette tape or compact disc stores. There are even video tapes with scenes and music that can assist with relaxation. These products are designed to help produce the deep relaxation we have described here. While we make no claims about their effectiveness, it is worth your time to check out a few for yourself to see how you respond.

If you are searching for audio cassettes or discs, there are environmental sounds which may be of interest to you. Also, some of the best instrumental music for relaxation are the many albums located in the "New Age" section.

19

Stress Relief: Eating Habits

— Laura Boenisch Zubrod, BS in Dietetics

*A*h, food! A great way to forget your troubles and be happy — or so it seems. Actually, *good* nutrition *can* be a way of reducing stress, but, unfortunately, we tend to eat the wrong things. The result: *more* stress, not less. In this chapter, we'll take a look at why.

Eating Your Way to Stress

Several major components of the typical American diet are, in the unfortunate proportions we usually consume them, potentially more harmful than good. Sugar, for example, is one which can be a major contributor to stress.

It surprised us to learn that approximately twenty-four percent of calories consumed by the average American is from sugars. And another thirty-seven percent is loaded with fats. Although both sugar and fat do provide certain limited nutritional elements for our bodies, we consume on the average far more than we need for optimum health — and that is the problem.

Quick Guide #6
Your Eating Habits

Rate yourself on the following items: ALWAYS   NEVER

	ALWAYS				NEVER
1. I eat a variety of foods.	5	4	3	2	1
2. I maintain my recommended weight.	5	4	3	2	1
3. I limit consumption of fat, saturated fat, and cholesterol.	5	4	3	2	1
4. I limit consumption of sugar.	5	4	3	2	1
5. I drink alcoholic beverages in moderation.	5	4	3	2	1
6. I eat foods with adequate complex carbohydrates and fiber.	5	4	3	2	1
7. I eat a healthy intake of fruits and vegetables.	5	4	3	2	1
8. I limit intake of pickled, salt-cured, smoked, and charred foods.	5	4	3	2	1
9. I protect myself from too much sun.	5	4	3	2	1
10. I avoid smoking.	5	4	3	2	1
11. I exercise regularly.	5	4	3	2	1
12. I limit consumption of sodium.	5	4	3	2	1

How did you do? The higher your score is above 48, the more you are in tune with healthy habits for your body. Much below 36? Please read this chapter!

Note: These items are based on the 1955 Dietary Guidelines for Americans published jointly by the U.S. Department of Agriculture (USDA) and U.S. Department of Health and Human Services (HHS).

If you are beginning to think that the average American eating habits can be a disaster, you are beginning to get the picture! But how do you know what to eat or what to avoid? Are there areas of a diet which are more harmful than others? Where should you begin? When the "experts" cannot agree, how are you to know what is best?

One sensible way is to slowly start changing those eating habits it has taken you years to form. Try alternative food products. Eat unprocessed, fresh food. Experiment with new ways of preparing and serving dishes; there are lots of healthy and easy recipes in cookbooks or magazines. Gradually reduce the more harmful items and just gradually increase the use of healthier foods until you and/or your family members get the taste of the new items. Variety, proportionality, and moderation are the keys. As you begin to change and learn more about nutrition, other modifications will seem appropriate.

The food guide pyramid is a helpful way to help guide you toward a healthy and balanced diet. Following a diet that includes variety, balance, and moderation will keep your body healthy and increase its resistance to distress. The foods at the base of the pyramid are the foods you should eat the most and the foods at the top should be used sparingly. No one group is more important than another; they are all needed for good health.

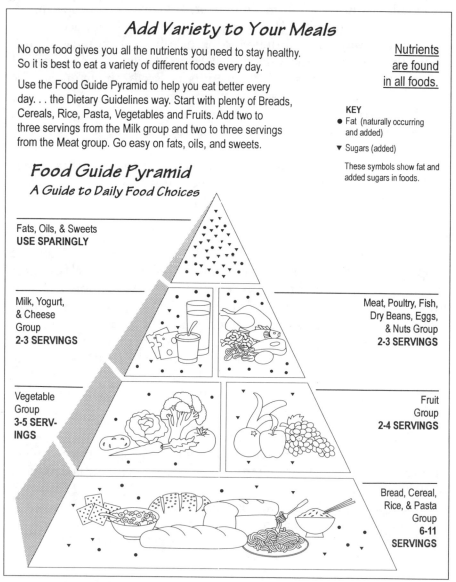

Add Variety to Your Meals

No one food gives you all the nutrients you need to stay healthy. So it is best to eat a variety of different foods every day.

Use the Food Guide Pyramid to help you eat better every day. . . the Dietary Guidelines way. Start with plenty of Breads, Cereals, Rice, Pasta, Vegetables and Fruits. Add two to three servings from the Milk group and two to three servings from the Meat group. Go easy on fats, oils, and sweets.

<u>Nutrients are found in all foods.</u>

KEY
● Fat (naturally occurring and added)
▼ Sugars (added)

These symbols show fat and added sugars in foods.

Food Guide Pyramid
A Guide to Daily Food Choices

Fats, Oils, & Sweets
USE SPARINGLY

Milk, Yogurt, & Cheese Group
2-3 SERVINGS

Meat, Poultry, Fish, Dry Beans, Eggs, & Nuts Group
2-3 SERVINGS

Vegetable Group
3-5 SERV-INGS

Fruit Group
2-4 SERVINGS

Bread, Cereal, Rice, & Pasta Group
6-11 SERVINGS

To assist you, examples of serving sizes within each group are listed below:

Bread Group: 1 slice of bread, 1/2 a hamburger bun, bagel or English muffin; 1/2 cup cooked cereal or granola type cereal, 1/2 cup rice or pasta, 1 cup ready-to-eat cereal, 4 small crackers, 1 tortilla.

Vegetable Group: 1/2 cup cooked or raw, chopped vegetables, 1 cup leafy raw vegetables, 3/4 cup vegetable juice.

Fruit Group: 1 whole medium fruit, 1/2 banana, 1/2 cup canned, chopped or cooked fruit; 1/4 cup dried fruit, 3/4 cup fruit juice.

Meat Group: 2 to 3 ounces cooked lean meat, poultry, or fish (about the size of a deck of cards), 1/2 cup cooked beans, 2 eggs, 4 tablespoons peanut butter, 1/2 cup nuts or seeds (high in fat, use sparingly), 7 ounces tofu.

Milk Group: 1 cup milk or yogurt, 1 1/2 ounces natural cheese, 2 ounces processed cheese, 1 1/2 cup frozen yogurt, ice milk or ice cream, 2 cups cottage cheese.

Use fats, oils, and sweets sparingly! Examples include: butter, salad dressing, mayonnaise, creamy or sweet sauces, vegetable oils, candy, desserts, alcohol.

Food Labels

Food labels have recently been changed to make them more complete, accurate, and useful to consumers. Using food labels can help you make healthy choices that may reduce diet related stressors and your risk factors for some diseases. In order to fully use food labels to your benefit, you must understand the information the label gives you. The following are the components of the typical label, an explanation of each, and a sample label. In addition to the new food label format, the meaning of words on food labels is now regulated by law. These standard definitions help you as a consumer know what you are getting or aren't getting in the foods you buy.

Key Words and What They Mean

Light, Lite. One-third fewer calories or 50% less fat per serving. If more than half the calories are from fat, the fat content must be reduced by 50% or more.

Low calorie. 40 calories or less per serving.

Calorie free. Less than 5 calories per serving.

Sugar free. Less than 1/2 gram of sugar per serving.

Nutrition Facts

Serving Size 1/2 cup (114g)
Servings Per Container 4

Amount Per Serving

Calories 90	Calories from Fat 30

	% Daily Value*
Total Fat 3g	5%
Saturated Fat 0g	0%
Cholesterol 0mg	0%
Sodium 300mg	13%
Total Carbohydrate 13g	4%
Dietary Fiber 3g	12%
Sugars 3g	
Protein 3g	

Vitamin A	80%	•	Vitamin C	60%
Calcium	4%	•	Iron	4%

* Percent Daily Values are based on a 2,000 calorie diet. Your daily values may be higher or lower depending on your calorie needs:

	Calories	2,000	2,500
Total Fat	Less than	65g	80g
Sat Fat	Less than	20g	25g
Cholesterol	Less than	300mg	300mg
Sodium	Less than	2,400mg	2,400mg
Total Carbohydrate		300g	375g
Fiber		25g	30g

Calories per gram:
Fat 9 • Carbohydrate 4 • Protein 4

More nutrients may be listed on some labels.

Serving Size

Is your serving the same size as the one on the label? If you eat double the serving size listed, you need to double the nutrient and calorie values. If you eat one-half the serving size shown here, cut the nutrient and calorie values in half.

Calories

Are you overweight? Cut back a little on calories! Look here to see how a serving of the food adds to your daily total. A 5' 4", 138-lb. active woman needs about 2,200 calories each day. A 5' 10", 174-lb. active man needs about 2,900. How about you?

Total Carbohydrate

When you cut down on fat, you can eat more carbohydrates. Carbohydrates are in foods like bread, potatoes, fruits and vegetables. Choose these often! They give you more nutrients than **sugars** like soda pop and candy.

Dietary Fiber

Grandmother called it "roughage," but her advice to eat more is still up-to-date! That goes for both soluble and insoluble kinds of dietary fiber. Fruits, vegetables, whole-grain foods, beans and peas are all good sources and can help reduce the risk of heart disease and cancer.

Protein

Most Americans get more protein than they need. Where there is animal protein, there is also fat and cholesterol. Eat small servings of lean meat, fish and poultry. Use skim or low-fat milk, yogurt and cheese. Try vegetable proteins like beans, grains and cereals.

Vitamins & Minerals

Your goal here is 100% of each for the day. Don't count on one food to do it all. Let a combination of foods add up to a winning score.

Total Fat

Aim low: Most people need to cut back on fat! Too much fat may contribute to heart disease and cancer. Try to limit your **calories from fat**. For a healthy heart, choose foods with a big difference between the total number of calories and the number of calories from fat.

Saturated Fat

A new kind of fat? No — saturated fat is part of the total fat in food. It is listed separately because it's the key player in raising blood cholesterol and your risk of heart disease. Eat less!

Cholesterol

Too much cholesterol — a second cousin to fat — can lead to heart disease. Challenge yourself to eat less than 300 mg each day.

Sodium

You call it "salt," the label calls it "sodium." Either way, it may add up to high blood pressure in some people. So, keep your sodium intake low — 2,400 to 3,000 mg or less each day.*

*The AHA recommends no more than 3,000 mg sodium per day for healthy adults.

Daily Value

Feel like you're drowning in numbers? Let the Daily Value be your guide. Daily Values are listed for people who eat 2,000 or 2,500 calories each day. If you eat more, your personal daily value may be higher than what's listed on the label. If you eat less, your personal daily value may be lower.

For fat, saturated fat, cholesterol and sodium, choose foods with a low **% Daily Value**. For total carbohydrate, dietary fiber, vitamins and minerals, your daily value goal is to reach 100% of each.

g = grams (About 28 g = 1 ounce)
mg = milligrams (1,000 mg = 1 g)

No sugar added. No sugar or ingredient containing sugar is added. The product contains no ingredients that contain added sugars, such as jam, jelly, concentrated fruit juice. The product it resembles and is substituted for normally contains added sugar.

Fat free. Less than 1/2 gram of fat per serving.

Low fat. 3 grams or less of fat per serving

__% fat free. Meets the requirements for a low fat food. The percentage is based on the amount of fat by weight in 100 grams of the food. For example, 50 grams of food containing 2 1/2 grams of fat can be labeled as 95% fat free.

Reduced fat. At least 25% less fat when compared with a similar food.

Cholesterol free. Less than 2 milligrams of cholesterol per serving and 2 grams or less of saturated fat per serving.

Low cholesterol. 20 milligrams or less of cholesterol per serving and 2 grams or less of saturated fat per serving.

Sodium or salt free. Less than 5 milligrams of sodium per serving.

Very low sodium. 35 milligrams or less of sodium per serving.

Low sodium. Has 140 milligrams or less of sodium per serving.

Unsalted, no added salt. No salt is added during processing. This does not mean the product is sodium free, there may be salt present naturally. The label will state if it is not a sodium free food.

Lean. Packaged seafood, game meat, cooked meat, or cooked poultry with less than 10 grams total fat, 4.5 grams or less of saturated fat, and less than 95 milligrams of cholesterol per 100 gram serving.

Extra lean. Packaged seafood, game meat, cooked meat, or cooked poultry with less than 5 grams total fat, less than 2 grams saturated fat, and less than 95 milligrams of cholesterol per 100 gram serving.

Good source of, Contains, Provides. Contains 10% to 19% of the Daily Value per serving. For example, a good source of iron is a food that contains 10% of the RDI (Recommended Daily Intake) which is 18 mg.

High, Rich in, Excellent source of. Contains 20% or more of the Daily Value per serving. For example, and excellent source of calcium provides 200 milligrams or more of calcium per serving.

More, Fortified, Enriched, Added. Contains at least 10% or more of the Daily Value for one or more of the following: protein, vitamins, minerals, dietary fiber, or potassium.

Serving Size. Similar foods now have standard serving sizes, such as ready-to-eat cereals, which makes comparing nutrients easier. Make sure your serving size matches the serving size listed. Double portions mean the nutrient and calorie values double also.

Calories. Tells how much energy the food provides.

Calories from Fat. This value helps you see how fatty a food is. There is a big difference between calories and calories from fat. Balance high fat foods with lower fat choices to keep your total fat intake to 30% or less of your total caloric intake.

Total Fat. Aim low! A good rule of thumb is to keep individual foods at thirty percent fat or lower, this means there should be no more than 3 grams of fat per 100 calories.

Saturated Fat. This value is part of the total fat value. It tells you how many of the total fat grams are from saturated fat. It is listed separately because saturated fat raises blood cholesterol and your risk of heart disease.

Cholesterol. Too much cholesterol can lead to heart disease. Cholesterol is only found in foods from animal sources such as milk, cheese, eggs, and meats. Keep daily consumption at 300 milligrams or less.

Sodium. Also called salt. It can increase blood pressure in some people. Aim low here, too: 2,400 to 3,000 milligrams or less per day.

Total Carbohydrate. Complex carbohydrates include foods such as bread, potatoes, fruits, and vegetables. Choose these often. Simple carbohydrates include sugars.

Dietary Fiber. Fiber is found in fruits, vegetables, whole-grain foods, beans and peas. Foods rich in fiber help reduce the risk of heart disease and cancer.

Sugars. These include table sugar as well as other forms of sugar such as corn syrup, honey, fruit sugars, etc. Sugars provide calories and no nutrients.

Protein. Protein is usually found in the company of fat and cholesterol. Most Americans get more protein than they need. Check out the Food Guide Pyramid. Use skim milk and other low-fat dairy products, lean meats, and other sources of protein such as beans, grains, and tofu.

Vitamins and Minerals. The goal here is to reach 100% for the day. The vitamins and minerals listed on the label will vary according to the food. Food combining is the way to go; one food source cannot provide all the vitamins and minerals your body needs.

Percent Daily Value. This is based on a 2,000 calorie diet. It tells the amount of each nutrient provided as a percentage of 2,000 calories.

If you eat more, the percent daily value will be higher. The only values that will change along with calories are total fat, saturated fat, and total carbohydrate. Cholesterol, sodium, and dietary fiber amounts are the same for everyone.

Calories per gram This may not appear on all labels. It is basically a key to the caloric amounts listed on the label. Each gram of fat provides 9 calories and one gram of carbohydrate and protein each provide 4 calories. For example, multiplying the number of fat grams by 9 will tell you how many calories are from fat.

You should become aware of four areas of your diet which, if they are present in excess, can cause the most potential harm over the years: CAFFEINE, SUGAR, SALT, and FAT. Over-consumption (and most Americans do!) can lead to potentially dangerous illnesses and trigger physiological reactions which are very similar to some of the reactions in a stress response (Chapter 1). Life usually produces enough situations that can result in anxiety, tension and distress. Doesn't it seem just a little unusual, maybe even crazy, to be eating your way to *more* distress?

The Great American Distress Break

Several times each day millions of Americans unknowingly create unnecessary distress responses in themselves. The irony is that these people are involved in a national ritual that is supposed to produce both mental and physical relaxation: the coffee break.

The ten to fifteen minute break from work is a fairly standard morning and afternoon ritual. The most common ingredients include coffee or tea, a light "energizing" snack of pie, cake, rolls, candy bars, cookies, salted peanuts or chips. It is not uncommon for a cigarette to appear sometime during the break. The only thing wrong with that is... EVERYTHING! Despite minor variations, the ingredients usually include *caffeine, sugar, salt, fat, and nicotine.*

Caffeine is a stimulant drug. In moderate amounts it can exhilarate, energize, and increase alertness and performance of many motor skills. The effects are normally felt within thirty minutes and will last for about three hours. In excessive amounts, however, caffeine can cause sweating, nervousness, jumpiness and anxiety. It also increases the secretion of stomach acids, reduces levels of blood sugar resulting in hunger, leads to sleeplessness, and could cause headaches, heartburn, heart disease, bleeding ulcers, and possible cancer of the bladder and pancreas.

Coffee is the most common source of caffeine, but not the only one. Most carbonated drinks, tea and chocolate contain caffeine. Consider the following chart and keep in mind the intakes of more than 250 mg per day are considered excessive.

Eating Habits

Item	Caffeine Content
*Excedrin (1 tablet)	65 mg
Soft drinks (12 oz)	32-65 mg
Coffee (5 oz)	66-146 mg
Tea (5 oz)	20-46 mg
Cocoa (5 oz)	13 mg
Chocolate candy (1 oz)	20 mg

Sources: *Journal of the American Dietetic Association, American Journal of Psychiatry*

*Source: Product label

Analyze your caffeine consumption. Is it excessive? What is your body telling you when you have too much? Slowly start decreasing your intake level until it is consistently below 250 mg per day. If you want to give up caffeine, investigate decaffeinated coffees, non-coffee grain beverages, name-brand herbal teas and juices. Read labels carefully and give your body time to wean itself from this drug.

The typical stress response affects your whole body from pituitary to pulse rate. Distress is usually caused by an atypical situation: waking up late, a dead battery, and IRS audit letter, a near traffic accident, a quarrel, a raise, a new job. A stress reaction can be beneficial and helpful in an emergency. The chemistry of your body creates an internal force that can continue helping you as long as you need to cope with the life event. But a stress response unknowingly and artificially created by the "Great American Coffee Break" — more appropriately called the "Great American Distress Break" — is of more harm than benefit. When compared to the standard stress response, the effects of caffeine and its common companions sugar and nicotine, can produce high levels of tension and anxiety — and very little renewal when you return to work after your break!

The Sugar You Did Not Know You Bought

In the late 1800's, Americans consumed an average of forty pounds of sugar per person per year. Seem like a lot? It is, especially when you consider that sugar in an "empty" food which provides calories but does little nutritionally for your body. Vitamins, minerals, fiber and protein are virtually absent. Speculate about the *current* per capita of sugar consumption while we tell you more about sugar.

The only good thing that can be said about sucrose (the chemical name for refined sugar, brown sugar, and honey) is that it provides a quick source of energy. Your body converts the sucrose into a simpler substance known as glucose which is the source of energy used by the body's cells. In addition, glucose is converted into glycogen, a source of future energy which is stored in the muscles and liver until needed. But the quick energy of sugar is not such a great benefit. Other foods such as fresh fruits, fresh vegetables, whole grain breads and cereals, pasta, and dried beans and peas can provide the same energy levels as sugar. What's more, their contributions are of sustained value. Sugar's quick pick up disappears as fast as it comes. Even more important, these foods supply vitamins, minerals, and fiber; sucrose does not.

Not only is sucrose of little *use* to the body, when consumed in typical American diet excess it can be *harmful*. The most obvious problem is that a high intake of sugar results in a lot of calories. If the calories are not "burned" through physical activity, they are stored as fat and obesity can result. Consumption of both refined and natural sugars in excessive quantities has been linked to tooth and gum problems, raised levels of blood fats, kidney irregularities, blood pressure fluctuations and insulin imbalances.

If other foods can provide the benefits without undesirable side effects, why would anyone continue to distress the body by eating sugar? The American diet is partially to blame. Sugar has become more widely used since the turn of the century. Now the average yearly consumption of sugar is — are you ready — *128 pounds*, with children gobbling up closer to *140 pounds!*

The amount of sugar we consume has dramatically increased partly because of commercial food processing methods. It is very difficult to find any type of commercially-prepared food that does not contain sugar. It is also present in so many tempting and habit-forming goodies such as jams and jellies, candies, gums, cakes, cookies, pies, custards, cobblers, puddings, syrups, toppings, ice creams, sherbets, donuts, sundaes, milk shakes and on and on. Many find it hard to imagine an all-American meal without a dessert of at least one of these items.

The hidden sugars in our "processed diet" make it hard to stay away from sugar even if you *want* to! Sugar is not only used in sweet baked goods but also in soft drinks, almost all fruit drinks, some baby foods, salad dressings, canned and dehydrated soups, frozen vegetables, most canned and frozen fruits and breakfast cereals. If you eat a hot-dog, there is sugar in the meat, catsup, relish, mayonnaise, mustard, bun and even the chili if you go all the way!

Breakfast cereals are a real shocker. A study of seventy-eight brands was reported in the *Journal of Dentistry for Children*. Shredded Wheat® had the lowest with only one percent sucrose content. The percentages rose to a high of sixty-eight percent! The sugar content of candy ranges from thirty-nine percent to ninety-seven percent. The average sucrose content of the dry cereals was twenty-five percent. Eat a breakfast of pre-sweetened cereal, sweetened fruit juice, toast with jelly or a roll and the level of sugar in this critical meal could easily approach thirty to forty percent.

Cutting down on sugar takes effort and vigilance. It also takes acquiring a new taste for the exciting natural sweetness already in foods. Read labels. You will be amazed at how many processed foods in your daily diet contain sugar — almost every one. Food labels have become easier to read since the FDA created a new label. Every new food label now lists the number of grams and percent daily value of total carbohydrate found in the food. Total carbohydrates are also broken down in to dietary fiber and sugars. This makes it very easy to determine how much sugar is in the product. The amount of sugar listed on the label includes *all* sugars: dextrose, glucose, maltose, fructose, lactose, galactose, levulose, corn syrup, honey, corn sugar, and molasses. Fruit juice concentrate is likely to be high in sugar if one of the previous terms appears first or second in the ingredients list, or if several of them are listed.

With so much sugar already in your food, it is not practical or possible to totally eliminate the consumption of "empty" or unneeded sugar calories. But you can follow a few suggestions for cutting down.

• In place of sweet snacks or candy, substitute popcorn, raw vegetables or fruits for the munchies. It really helps if the vegetables are already cut up and stored in the refrigerator, readily accessible for a quick and easy snack.

• Get in the habit of serving fresh fruit for dessert. If you must rely on canned or frozen fruit, choose those packed in water instead of sweet syrup.

• Instead of buying cakes, pies or cookies, make your own. Try reducing the sugar in the recipe a little more each time you bake. The sugar in most recipes can be reduced by one-third without really affecting the taste.

• Make dessert breads that contain little sugar but are loaded instead with nourishing ingredients like whole wheat flour, oatmeal, nuts, raisins, cranberries, orange peels or carrots.

• Reward children with attention, privileges, gifts, fruit, nuts — *not sweets*!

• If you put sugar in coffee or tea, gradually reduce the amount you use until you become accustomed to not using it at all. Then go to work on cutting down the caffeinated coffee or tea itself!

• Eliminate soft drinks from your diet. Try other refreshing drinks such as mineral water, unsweetened vegetable or fruit juices or spring water with a twist of lemon, lime or orange.

• Purchase dry cereals that have less than ten percent sugar (3 grams per 1 oz. serving) and use fresh or dried fruits to provide the sweet flavor you may crave.

• Alternative sweeteners such as saccharin, acesulfame-k, aspartame (NutraSweet®), and sugar alcohols (xylitol, sorbitol, mannitol) are found in a variety of foods such as chewing gum, soft drinks, juices, candy, pudding and Jell-O® mixes, etc. Sorbitol is the only sugar substitute thus far that has been shown to cause cancer. Foods with alternative sweeteners are an excellent way to still enjoy those foods you love without the added calories from sugar. However, these foods, like all sweets should be consumed in moderation. There is little evidence of the effects of excessive consumption of alternative sweeteners.

• Be aware that fat-free products are often high in sugar and calories. Read labels and be conscious of these trade-offs. The original product, when compared to the fat-free or low-fat version, may be the healthier choice.

Salt Preserves Your Food But Not Your Body

Salt plays many roles. It enhances flavors, controls ripening and bacterial growth in cheese and fruit, and preserves fermented foods like pickles. Many canned and processed foods are washed or stored in brine.

The sodium provided by salt is a very necessary element for proper body functioning, as are dozens of other chemicals. But like those other chemicals, too much can be damaging. Your body does not need a large amount of salt. The Recommended Daily Allowance (RDA) for sodium is 500 milligrams per day, which is the minimum your body needs to function properly. The American Heart Association recommends that you keep your sodium between 2,400 to 3,000 milligrams per day or less. It is estimated that the average American consumption is between 6,000 and 18,000 milligrams per day, but could be as high as 40,000 milligrams per day. Without adding any salt, the average consumption is about 5,000 milligrams. Using the salt shaker can increase salt consumption significantly. One teaspoon of table salt (sodium chloride) contains approximately 2,000 milligrams of sodium. Many foods contain enough sodium naturally to meet most daily requirements. The excess consumption occurs when foods are processed with salt, cooked with salt, and then more salt is added at the table.

Some of the food processing ingredients which contain sodium are monosodium glutamate or MSG (flavor enhancer), sodium saccharin (sweetener), sodium phosphate (stabilizer and buffer), sodium citrate (buffer), sodium caseinate (thickener and binder) and sodium benzoate and sodium nitrate (preservatives). Some common additives, although usually used in small quantities, are also high in sodium and should be avoided whenever possible: soy sauce, Worcestershire sauce, catsup, pickles, olives, garlic salt, onion salt, celery salt, baking soda, baking powder, monosodium glutamate and meat tenderizers containing salt.

To make matters worse, many foods that do not taste salty may still contain large amounts of sodium. Different varieties of the same food product may contain less sodium naturally or as a result of different processing methods.

In general, foods in their natural state contain very little sodium but still enough to meet human daily requirements. Frozen vegetables are usually processed without added salt. However, vegetables with added sauces or nuts are higher in sodium, fat and calories than the plain variety. Canned vegetables are usually packed in a salt solution. There are low sodium canned vegetables available. Or rinsing canned vegetables and beans will remove some of the salt but not all of it. Salted or brined meats and fish are obviously higher in salt content than uncured forms. Even the water softener in your home is a hidden source: it substitutes sodium for the minerals in hard water. The chart on page 144 lists some foods high in sodium and comparable foods with much less sodium.

Sodium Level Comparisons

	LOW SODIUM LEVELS		HIGH SODIUM LEVELS		
Food	Serving	Sodium (milligrams)	Sodium (milligrams)	Serving	Food
Cheddar cheese	1 oz	176	457	4 oz	Cottage cheese (reg. & low fat)
Mozzarella	1 oz	106	528	1 oz	Grated Parmesan
Natural Swiss	1 oz	74	388	1 oz	Pasteurized Swiss
Sardines	3 oz	522	5234	3 oz	Smoked herring
Raw shrimp	3 oz	137	1955	3 oz	Canned shrimp
Cooked lean beef	3 oz	55	1114	3 oz	Ham
Chicken breast	1/2 breast	69	220	1 slice	Beef bologna
Peanuts (unsalted)	1 cup	8	986	1 cup	Peanuts (dry roasted, salted)
Pecans	1 cup	1	1200	1 cup	Cashews (dry roasted, salted)
English walnuts	1 cup	3			
Pistachios	1 cup	6			
Green beans (frozen)	1 cup	7	326	1 cup	Green beans (canned)
Corn (fresh cooked)	1 ear	1	385	1 cup	Corn (canned, regular, whole kernel)
Mushrooms (raw)	1 cup	7	968	1 cup	Mushrooms (canned)
Green peas (fresh cooked)	1 cup	2	493	1 cup	Green peas (canned)
Tomato paste	1 cup	77	1498	1 cup	Tomato sauce
Garlic powder	1 tsp	1	1850	1 tsp	Garlic salt
			1152	1 cup	Beef broth (cubed)
Popcorn (plain)	1 cup	1	.75	1 cup	Popcorn (oil, salted)

Source: U.S. Department of Agriculture, Bulletin 233, August 1980.

Why should you be concerned with the level of sodium in your diet? Try these three compelling reasons:

• You are probably like most Americans who consume too much salt every day.

• Most salt is "hidden" and results in unknown and high levels of salt consumption. Fortunately the new food labels now list the amount of salt present in foods. Label reading will help you target the high sources of salt in your diet.

• The most important reason for carefully monitoring and restricting sodium intake is because health and life may depend on it. After years of consuming too much salt, the body's mechanism for maintaining proper levels gradually becomes less efficient. As more sodium is retained, more water is retained to dilute the sodium. Blood volume increases, gradually placing more and more strain on the arteries and heart. Blood pressure gradually rises in those susceptible to this silent killer. Hypertension, cardiovascular problems and early death could result.

The most harmful effects of excessive salt consumption do not show up for years. The medical community cannot predict who will be endangered by high sodium diets before the damage is done. This means it is up to you to accept the dangers of a high salt diet and start changing now. Therefore, everyone is encouraged to consume no more than 2,400 milligrams per day.

The steps are easy and inexpensive:

• Become conscious of daily salt intake by reading labels and learning of the hidden sources of salt.

• Start to reduce and eventually eliminate the addition of salt in cooking and at the table.

• Learn to use herbs and spices in place of salt. Dry mustard, garlic powder, celery, celery powder and allspice are good examples. The are also many salt-free seasonings available. Depending on the food, a large number of other spices could be used in place of salt. An excellent resource is a booklet available through the American Heart Association: *Cooking Without Your Salt Shaker*.

The Fat of the Land

About thirty-seven percent of the typical American diet consists of fats from sources such as meats, butter, eggs, whole milk, cheeses, dessert and snack foods, and fast food. The average American consumes from six to eight tablespoons of fat each day, yet we need only *one* tablespoon for balanced nutrition — and sometimes not even that much. The total level of fat in the diet that virtually all health organizations recommend is thirty percent or less with no more than one-third coming from saturated fat. Ideally twenty to twenty-five percent would be best but it is difficult to maintain.

The major health concern is with those fats which tend to increase cholesterol levels in the blood stream. Cholesterol is a substance obtained only from animal products such as meat, milk, cheese, butter, and eggs. Vegetable oils and margarines prepared from vegetable oils do not contain cholesterol. It is used by your cells to produce sex hormones, vitamin D, strong cell membranes and protective sheaths around your nerves. The liver produces over 1,000 milligrams of cholesterol each day to meet these needs. No additional cholesterol is needed, yet the average American diet dumps an additional 450 milligrams into the body. It is recommended that you get no more than 300 milligrams of cholesterol per day. One egg yolk has 208 milligrams of cholesterol!

Excess cholesterol travels through the blood stream, clinging to the artery walls, and gradually closing them off. After a number of years, excessive fat consumption takes its toll in the form of atherosclerosis, heart attacks, strokes, and obesity.

Saturated fats are the major villain in this drama, since it is this group which contributes to increased blood cholesterol. Examples of saturated fats, which should be minimized, include butter, cheeses made with whole milk, cream, palm oil, coconut and coconut oil, egg yolks, lard, meat fats, whole milk, poultry fat and vegetable shortening. One key to spotting and recognizing many undesirable saturated fats is that they will be firmer and more solid at room temperature. The food labels now list the percentage of saturated fat contained in foods.

A second type, *monounsaturated* fats, are classified into a "neutral" category. These include avocados, cashews, olives and olive oil, peanut butter, peanuts and peanut oil. Because these fats are less harmful does not mean that you can eat more of them, they still have the same amount of calories. Rather, these fats should be substituted for saturated fats in your diet.

The last type, polyunsaturated fats, used to be considered the most helpful fats because they decrease blood cholesterol levels. These fats lower the bad LDL (low density lipoproteins) as well as the good HDL (high density lipoproteins). We now know that low levels of HDL could be just as much a risk factor for heart disease as high levels of LDL. Also, high amounts of polyunsaturated fats can increase the risk of several types of cancer.

Recently *trans* fatty acids have become a health concern. *Trans* fatty acids are formed by hydrogenation or the addition of hydrogen atoms to polyunsaturated fats such as those listed above. Hydrogenation makes liquid oils more solid and stable and, for example, gives margarine its creamy texture. However, hydrogenation also makes unsaturated oils more saturated by changing their structure and therefore they are called *trans* fatty acids. These *trans* fatty acids may have the same damaging effects as saturated fats. So what do you do? Should you avoid margarine and go back to butter? The best alternative is to cut back on margarine and try liquid margarines, the more liquid, the less hydrogenation. Diet margarines are also a good alternative because they contain water and about half the fat as regular margarine.

The fat you consume is not the whole story. It is not the blood cholesterol levels alone that are of concern. More important are the proportions of HDL and LDL in blood cholesterol and how the various fats we eat affect these levels.

Research lays blame for high blood pressure and other stress- related health problems with smoking, obesity, inactivity, environmental conditions and other factors. It is clearly a complex phenomenon! Nevertheless, reduced fat consumption appears to be one very important and relatively easy step you can take toward better health and reduced distress. We urge you to consider these suggestions for gradually learning to live with less fat:

- Trim excess fat from meats; skin poultry before cooking.
- Select fish, poultry, lean meats, dry beans and peas as your protein sources.
- "Select" grades of meat are leaner than "prime" or "choice."
- Limit your consumption of eggs, try egg substitutes, use only the egg whites (2 whites = 1 egg).
- Prepare foods by baking, broiling, grilling, steaming, roasting, poaching.
- Eat more fruits and vegetables.
- Substitute applesauce for oil in baking.
- Refrigerate canned and homemade soups and stews overnight and remove fat that congeals on the surface.
- Use non-stick cooking sprays for baking.
- Sauté in a non-stick pan with little or no oil.

- Use evaporated skim milk in place of cream or half-and-half in recipes.
- When eating out, avoid dishes described as: buttery, crispy, creamy, basted, sautéed, fried, au gratin, escalloped, hollandaise, marinated, and prime.
- Use low fat dairy products and skim milk.
- Read labels! Look for the amount of fat from calories. A good rule is to have no more than 3 grams of fat per 100 calories (30% fat).

Healthy Snack Suggestions

Don't get depressed with all this information on sugars, fats, caffeine and salt. There is hope. Here are some ideas to help you cope with the munchies. Only eat a snack if you are hungry. You do not have to eat during your coffee break. Instead, read a few pages in a novel, write a letter, meditate, take a quick walk. If you are indeed hungry, here are some healthy snack ideas:

Water: Plain water is always recommended. Your body needs lots of it on a regular basis. It is non-fattening and, if you drink a full glass before eating, it will help curb your appetite.

Fresh fruit: fruit salad, melon salad, bananas, apples, oranges, grapes, pears, peaches. When selecting canned fruit, choose lite syrup or natural juices. Dried fruit is a healthy snack but also high in calories.

Fresh vegetables: cucumber spears, broccoli, cauliflower, celery, carrots, mushrooms, radishes, tomatoes. Try dipping these in fat-free ranch dressing or making your favorite vegetable dip with non-fat yogurt or fat-free sour cream.

Low-fat cottage cheese. Plain or with fruit

Bagels. Spread with fat-free or low-fat cream cheese or jelly. Raisin bagels taste great plain! Watch out for those muffins; they are loaded with fat.

Non-fat yogurt. Try varieties with fruit added or buy plain and add your own fruit or dry cereal. Watch out for granola, it is very high in fat and calories. Look for low-fat granola or make your own.

Low-fat string cheese and other cheeses with less than 5 grams of fat per ounce.

Microwave popcorn. Read the label carefully, some varieties are loaded with fat.

Cookies. Try these low-fat varieties: fig bars, ginger snaps, vanilla wafers, graham crackers.

Crackers. These are lower in fat: matzo, melba toast, rye flatbread crackers, saltines.

Rice Cakes. They don't resemble cardboard any more! There are tons of great flavors.

Chips. There are now baked tortilla chips and fat-free potato chips available! Try a little salsa; it's no fat and lots of taste.

Pretzels. Low fat varieties are available.

Sugar-free gelatin desserts and pudding. Mix them up at home and bring them to work for a delicious snack.

Angel-food cake. Fat-free and great with fresh fruit.

Up in Smoke

Although not technically a *dietary* consideration, smoking and chewing tobacco has such clear effects on the body's stress levels that it deserves mention here.

Arteriosclerosis; bronchitis; emphysema; heart disease; high blood pressure; and cancer of the lung, larynx, lip, oral cavity, esophagus, bladder or other urinary organs are caused by smoking. Cigarettes, cigars, pipe smoking and chewing deplete the body of nutrients. Smoking blunts the ability to taste and smell. Other people are forced to breathe the dangerous gases, which permeate skin, hair, clothes and furniture. The nauseous odors are easily detected by non-smokers — but not by smokers.

Claims of smokers notwithstanding, smoking does not relax the body; it is a physical stimulant. Any relaxation from smoking is psychological — and very temporary! The only good thing which can be said about this dangerous and expensive crutch is, "I have kicked the habit!"

As prior smokers, it is easy for us (the authors) to acknowledge that stubbornness and keen ability to make excuses usually keep smokers from stopping. Since the early '60s when the Surgeon General first reported on the dangers of smoking, a continuous stream of reports have confirmed the hazards in books, articles, research papers, films, television specials.

Organizations such at the American Lung Association, the American Cancer Society, the American Heart Association and the National Institutes of Health produce an abundance of excellent information for anyone needing to be convinced to stop. Millions have successfully kicked the habit on their own, gradually, "cold turkey," or with the help of others through clinics and programs. The help is available; the research facts and statistics are becoming more overwhelming. What's your excuse for continuing this highly distressing and destructive habit?

On a Personal Level

Nearly all of the data we have presented in this chapter are based on large-scale studies and interpretations of what is "good for the average person." The toughest part of all of this is that *no one* is an "average person"!

A nutritional program which is optimum for you must take into account your age, sex, lifestyle, level of general health, physical activity, distress factors, temperament, any short-term illness, any chronic medical condition, and your medical history. There is no way we can offer in this book a recommended diet or eating plan which will take all these factors into account for every reader! Thus we urge you to carefully examine your own unique combination of the factors we have mentioned. Develop a systematic plan for improving the way food contributes to *reducing* your overall distress level! And remember, registered dieticians (RD) are a key resource. Ask your physician.

In summary, if you are like most Americans, you could have a healthier, more balanced and maybe longer life if you did the following:

Fats	decrease
Water	increase
Activity	increase
Salt	decrease
Sugar	decrease
Whole grains	increase
Fruits	increase
Vegetables	increase
Smoking	eliminate
Alcohol	decrease
Weight	decrease
Caffeine	decrease
Healthy snacks	increase

And always remember, have fun discovering how healthy you can be by practicing moderation!

20

Stress Relief: Physical Activity

Your body is like a finely tuned car. The engine will not even turn over if it has not periodically been started and let run. The tires will even look square after a while. Your body as well will not retain its functioning or tone if you leave fitness as part of your schedule until after retirement. Good physical fitness should actually start in childhood. Studies have shown that as early as six years old a body can begin to deteriorate. If you can start in early childhood, it then becomes a part of your lifestyle.

In managing stress more effectively and efficiently, you are able to achieve a new picture or inner self-image. Regular physical exercise will promote more vital physical health, more positive emotional states and more acute mental powers. The bottom line is that if you choose not to be physically fit, your capacity to do so will diminish with age. You may find that your "get up and go" has "got up and went."

Fatigue and loss of energy are usually the first lines of defense for bodies whose owners resist exercise. It makes sense; rest is an age-old prescription for exhaustion. But more often than not, increased rest alone does not dispel fatigue.

Like the food you eat and the environment that surrounds you, your choices in personal behavior shape your health. Research evidence shows that physical fitness can reduce the incidence of coronary disease, hypertension, overweight, boredom, depression, premature aging, lack of flexibility, poor musculature, mental tension and stress-related diseases. Americans, unfortunately, have bought into the "American Way of Life" and it is slowly but surely killing you and me. It is a lifestyle that is difficult to resist because it dominates society, and unless you have decided to become a hermit or a recluse, you are faced with fighting self-destructive behaviors.

At this point in your life you probably don't hunt for your food nor work to grow your food in the fields. The American lifestyle that was once so active has become tremendously sedentary. You probably spend a great deal of money on technology that will prevent you from having to use much physical energy. You no longer walk, but drive. Recreation has become relegated to the armchair. The problem is that your body was never designed to be sedentary. If your level of exercise is walking from the car to the house, now is the time to rethink your frame of mind.

The federal government initiated programs for federal employees based on evidence that fitness leads to reduced employee mortality. Examine the fifteen variables that contribute to someone's chances of suffering a heart attack:

blood pressure	EKG reading	fibrindysians
activity level	pulmonary function	cigarette smoking
blood sugar	heredity	uric acid
triglycerides	weight	glucose tolerance
mood & coping	diet	cholesterol

All but one (heredity) can be positively affected by exercising for twenty-five minutes a day!

Studies which have compared exercise to a widely prescribed tranquilizer found that exercise was superior in relaxing and elevating the individual's mood without any drug side effects. There is a general feeling of well-being that you have after a good physical workout. What runners describe as that feeling of "high" is related to euphoria.

As a bonus, it turns out that exercise is as good for your mind as it is for your body! It is also true that exercise delays the effects of aging as well as improves the body's ability to fight infection. What exercise and physical fitness can do is change your general attitude. Everyday problems seem less important, you tend to eat less, and need less sleep. In fact, the quality of your life is improved all around!

Even though physical fitness requires as much dedication and consistency as nutrition and rest, your exercise program can really be enjoyable. And if it isn't then you will not stick with it. However, a few words of caution before you join the "fitness boom." Do not exert beyond your limit. If you do too much too soon, you run the risks of injury or discouragement. If you are over thirty-five, pregnant, have some type of illness or are obese, check out your prospective fitness program with a physician. For many, physical fitness does not come easily, and unfortunately can not be swallowed like a pill or achieved by taking out a membership in your local health club. You need to put your own individual twist on your program. What you will develop is an overall behavior pattern, which can start as easily and as cheaply as walking around the block.

Getting Started

You need to remember that it will probably take at least a month for exercise to change your body, but it can change your mood immediately. No need to take Prozac.® Remember how it feels when you have been cooped up? It makes you feel cranky and old. Then you take a nice long walk and you can take a week's worth of stress out of your muscles. As you start your program of fitness, consider the following:

• *Set some goals.* You might even want to use a training log. Record what you want to do and then what you actually did do.

• *Warm up.* Do some warm-up stretching before exercising. This will prevent muscle pulls and unnecessary soreness. Most books on fitness give detailed examples of warm-up stretches.

• *Create rituals.* Whether you shake out your arms before swimming or shake out your legs before running, or check your shoe laces before walking, you may not improve your performance, but it will allow you to create a better mental connection. It is like taking those extra swings before you actually connect club to golf ball.

• *Make movies with your mind.* Even if you are sitting on a stationary bike, imagine what the riders in front of you look like. As you begin to tire, imagine yourself making it over that hill.

• *Talk yourself fit.* Forget all the negative thoughts. Instead of seeing yourself as a beached whale, see yourself as a playful dolphin.

Exercising in the late afternoon, after a day full of work, in or out of the house, or both, seems to promote a good night's sleep. Just be careful not to work out too vigorously a hour or two before bedtime as sleep might be difficult. Save that for the morning when you want to get the adrenaline flowing.

Among the best exercises to improve your cardiovascular system and improve your endurance are bicycling, walking, running and swimming. Our recommendation is to start with walking for ten minutes every other day for two weeks, fifteen minutes every other day the third week, and twenty minutes four to five times the fourth week. Gradually increase your pace, so that you are walking rapidly after a week or two. If you also meditate while you are walking, chances are that your resting heart rate and blood pressure will go down! After each workout, do some stretching exercises, have a glass of fresh fruit juice, take a shower and you are ready for anything. You will soon begin to discover new attitudes, feelings of positive self-esteem, less tension and more energy.

Getting Serious

• We hope you will "get hooked" on fitness and that it will become an important part of your everyday lifestyle. When this happens you will find yourself planning around your fitness schedule because it has become the most important part of your day.

• Discover what activity you do or like best. Analyze your body structure, environment, daily schedule, personal style, and present physical condition. You will know when it fits because you will actually have "withdrawal symptoms" when you miss it.

• Find your own type of play. When exercise becomes play, it becomes a self-renewing habit. Look at old skills from your childhood, adolescence or young adulthood. How have you played before?

• Realize that part of continuation in your fitness program is related to creating a climate of support for yourself. Getting serious about physical fitness requires some sacrifice. Pursuing any type of goal then becomes difficult if those around you are not supportive. Also realize that climate takes on a different focus when explained in geographical terms. Where you live and the climate of the region can either enhance or detract from certain types of physical fitness. Few places in the country can you ski year-round or play tennis year-round. On the bright side, a valuable side benefit of exercise is that you'll get in touch with Mother Nature. Exercise can be a good way to commune with the environment.

• Take a look at what your community has to offer: Health club programs, local college classes, Y activities, public recreation facilities.

• Don't think of fitness as a crash program. Go slowly and gradually.

• Fitness should be fun; don't cheat yourself by taking any physical activity too seriously. Competition can give you more stress! Don't have heroic expectations for yourself.

• A little activity goes a long way, so don't go overboard. Once you are "in shape," three twenty-minute sessions a week can maintain an adequate level of fitness for you, if the activity produces sustained cardiovascular effort.

• Learn to breathe correctly as you are exercising.

• Express your fitness objectives in a contract with yourself; set daily, weekly, and monthly goals.

• Realize that some activities, such as football, may only be enjoyed by the young and others are great for adults. Still others can be enjoyed no matter what stage of life's development you are in. Be sure that you commit to finding the new challenges and the new adventures. You may put aside some old favorites to try something new. But well-learned skills will never be forgotten.

Physical Fitness Target*

Those sports within the center have the greatest positive effect on your cardiovascular system. The farther from the center the activity is placed, the less the effect.

*Developed by Dr. Judy Jones, University of Northern Colorado.

21

Stress Relief:
Time Management

Time is of the essence. We have met the enemy and it is "hours"!

You function in a world that deals in deadlines, interruptions, shortages of time, and requirements for time that occur simultaneously. The challenge is how to organize the twenty-four hours that have been allocated to you just like it is allocated to everyone else. Improving your time utilization allows you to avoid crises and thus distress, gain a feeling of accomplishment, and live life effectively, not just spend it. Managing time effectively allows you again to enrich your life by balancing. Like the salary you make, you have some choices. You can save some, invest some, spend some, waste some or make more. The choices you make are based upon the effective techniques (actions) you learn to use as well as your attitude. Time-use strategy involves investigating and answering two important questions:

"Where does all my time go?" and

"How do I want to use my time?"

The time you save will be well worth it.

In answering the first question...

Devise a simple time log to keep a record of how you actually spend your time, hour-by-hour for a week. Don't procrastinate until that "typical week" arrives; start now! After the week is over, categorize your time into work, leisure, people, sleep, and maintenance (eating, errands, bathing, chores, dressing). Make up your own categories to fit your lifestyle if that is more helpful. Finally, add up the hours in each category. Is this really the way you want to spend your life?

Answering the second question, "How do I want to use my time?" is a tougher question!

Control of your time starts with planning on a daily basis and setting priorities. Only then can you give up feeling guilty about lost opportunities and tasks undone. For example: If you are spending too much time in housework or yardwork, ask yourself if it might be more worth your time and money to pay a neighborhood boy or girl (or your own children) to do it for you. If you are finding that you are doing office work at home in the evenings and weekends and do not have enough time with the family, concentrate on incorporating more effective time management techniques at work.

Look at the way you are wasting your time. Check out "interruptions" in the index of Lakein's *How to Get Control of Your Time and Your Life*. You probably will find that you waste your time in similar ways every day. Many people discover that they are their own worst time wasters. If so, remember it is easier to be assertive with yourself and change your habits than someone else's!

If procrastination is a primary time waster for you, begin to conquer it. Don't let "trying to be super perfect" paralyze you. If you decide to put everything off until it is definite, you won't get much done. Make it a practice not to avoid the most difficult problems. That will just insure that the hardest part will be left when you are the most exhausted! And everything else you do before the difficult problem is tackled, if it ever is, will probably be colored with dread.

Different people respond better to different time schedules. Perhaps you are a "morning person" and function best between 6 and 9 a.m.; don't expect everyone to function effectively at that time. Find out when you are your "superself" and plan your most important or challenging activities during that time. The time log can help you find your best time. When you find it, don't waste your best energy and time with trivia which can wait until you are not your most productive.

Control of your time starts with planning on a daily basis and setting your priorities. Here is a suggested list of time savers or actions you can consider as presented or modify to fit your situation. They won't conquer your issue with the enemy which may be in the form of your mind and its attitude; but, the following tips will help you manage your most valuable ally!

At Work

• Start with only one project at a time. Try to avoid clutter on your desk — it's distracting. After you have chosen a project, follow it through to the finish whenever possible. Then you avoid having to reacquaint yourself with those loose threads.

• Create an environment that is conducive to work. Exposure to noise that is unpredictable or uncontrollable will affect your behavior. You will become more aggressive, unable to concentrate as well as having difficulty effectively dealing with colleagues.

• Give yourself permission, or ask permission to leave the office early. Tell yourself that you deserve the time off to rejuvenate and relax.

• Encourage management to restructure the work environment to include flex-time, part-time and job-sharing. Ask if paternal as well as maternal leave is available.

• Be sure and warn people that you are running late or you think you could be late. They will appreciate not being surprised.

• Interruptions are the biggest bandit of time. One problem is recognizing an interruption before it occurs. Interruptions take away your time without a requisition.

• Don't hesitate to close the door (if you are fortunate enough to have one) to give yourself that fifteen minutes to one hour of quiet time. It is amazing what you can get done. And if you don't have a door, is there some place you can go for quiet time and concentrated (uninterrupted) work?

• Set appointments that you can control (going to the other person's office).

• Develop conversation-enders like, "You must be busy, so I'll be brief."

• With the advent of car phones, drive time can be more productive. Just remember to keep your eyes on the road.

• Take advantage of the latest features like fax machines, cordless phones, speaker phones, conference calls, voice mail, and E-mail.

• Arrange meetings with yourself anywhere, even in the bathtub.

• It is important to give yourself time as well as anybody else.

• Identify the outside influences that "steal" your time and then put yourself in control. Prevent them from occurring.

• Are you afraid to put anything away for fear that you will never discover it again? Does this apply to the *stuff* on your desk as well? Just how much of that *stuff* still holds value? Do ever feel just paralyzed by looking at your desk?

• Get organized! Commit your time and yourself to creating a list of everything that requires your attention that is still in piles. Half of everything in your life that is overwhelming you can probably be thrown away. The remainder can be placed in separate files or piles until you are ready to deal with the project.

• People who claim that they thrive on crisis may be fooling themselves. Could it possibly be that you have put off the inevitable until it becomes the crisis? The solution can be as easy as planning ahead so that crisis is not the usual way of doing business but the unusual. There is very little that happens in any given day that is life threatening.

• How do you handle the daily detours in your life? What do you do with the most productive time of your day (which for most of us is the morning hours)? Do you spend your entire morning in a less than productive meeting, or tackling the most difficult problem on your agenda? Do you make unimportant telephone calls or get into a social conversation? Sometimes one trivial chore will lead us to another and there goes the rest of the day. Closely look at your day and your choices. And then consider how much you blame everybody and everything else when you may be the major cause of your time problems.

• How do you find time when you need it? How about telling everyone that you are not coming in and then do. Your calendar is clear and no one is expecting you. Think what you can accomplish! Or reserve the conference room and meet yourself. Don't tell anyone where you have gone. Or how about just staying at home and just see how much you can accomplish?

• Monday morning meetings can be the biggest waste of the day or perhaps the entire week. This period of time is often chosen so that you can decide on the priorities for the week. Moving the meeting to midweek will allow review for activities that have occurred as well as sufficient time remaining in the week for additional planning.

• How do you plan for unplanned time? The best way to start is to flip through your calendar and find the time slots that you have not yet filled. Then draw a line through them with a strong message to yourself that you are not going to commit yourself to anything except what you really want to do. Maybe it is time to spend with family, friends or just yourself. What is really great is when you can just be spontaneous and do whatever you choose to do at the moment. Be sure that you don't let other people's demands get in your way. It is your gift to yourself.

• Are you putting your nose to the grindstone day in and day out? If so, maybe you need to be taking yourself less seriously and work less personally. Spend more time on your own needs...like being fit, eating and sleeping well and involving yourself in positive· personal relationships. You may find that the time you spend on other tasks will be more productive.

At Home

• Reward yourself after completing a task. Take a five to fifteen minute break and have a cup of decaf, read the comics, take a short walk or lie under a tree (if you are fortunate enough to be in a part of the world where this is possible). Do what feels good. The more you are comfortable with the idea of rewarding yourself for being organized, the more creative you will become with leisure activities.

• Organize your life as you would laundry. The whites (errands) in one pile, the dark colors (phone calls) in another. Priorities then become easier to identify.

• When you are planning a project, give yourself some breathing room. In other words, be sure you have given yourself extra time for cushioning. This applies when you are completing a project, driving across town, helping your children complete activities or making vacation travel arrangements. You know that rushing around "willy-nilly" adds to your stress level. So why rush? Build in some time.

• Some unplanned time needs to come on the weekend/vacation time so that you can regroup. Many of us plan to do all those things like housecleaning and yard maintenance in these time periods because we don't have time during the regular work week. With this type of scheduling, there is no relief in sight and you go back to work as exhausted as before.

• Open up a discussion with a friend about the "musts" and the "shoulds" that you spend a great deal of time fussing over. This could be a result of early family conditioning or gender "requirements" (e.g., "men mow lawns," "women wash clothes"). Whatever the origin, the fact that you perpetuate them extends your stress levels.

• Do you feel that your life is often times boring and unstimulating? Take the time to list the chores and tasks you are responsible for and the amount of time spent on these activities. Contrast these with amount of time spent on the activities of life that bring you joy. If there is an imbalance, seek balance.

• At home be aware of distractions which serve as interruptions such as noisy televisions, washing machines or barking dogs. Noise can make it extremely difficult to concentrate.

With Relationships

• Don't promise anyone anything until you know how much time this commitment involves. You owe it to yourself.

• When was the last time you said "no" to someone else and "yes" to yourself? It can be as simple as breaking the pattern of always saying "yes" and hating yourself later. Do you fall victim to the thought that you are the only one that can do it or everything will fall apart if you are not there?

• Procrastination is difficult but not impossible to get beyond. Often times it works when you have friends making you accountable, whether it is losing weight, getting involved with an exercise program, or finishing a knitting project. Call it peer pressure, one-upmanship or accountability, you just don't let your friends down. We like to call it loving support! This book was written thanks in part to the regular weekly phone calls of two colleagues who promised each other productivity.

• How do you react when someone asks, "How's your personal life?" Have you become so rigid that personal relationships, even marriage partners, have been excluded? Do people in your life, including your children, have to get on your calendar? You are proceeding toward burnout when you deprive yourself of emotions and feelings. So little time does not have to mean so little love. Very few of us "have it all" but we could have a little of each — again, balance.

Another Ninety-Five Ways to Save Time
At Home. . .

- Keep a bulletin board, with appointment calendar attached, near the phone. Schedule play time on your calendar so you will be sure to relax, create, exercise and be with friends regularly.
- File coupons and other papers in file boxes to maintain clean bulletin boards and desk tops.

- Use family or group time to brainstorm ideas for menus, vacation plans or new ways to budget.
- Put an asterisk beside each tax-deductible expenditure on your monthly budget sheet or in your checkbook. At tax time, simply transfer the items to one sheet.
- Pay a tax accountant to do your income tax.
- Keep a notebook in your car glove compartment for noting service and maintenance dates.
- Walk straight from your mailbox to the trash can to deposit junk mail.
- Put things away after using them.
- Make meals ahead of time and freeze them to use on heavy-scheduled days.
- Hire a high school student to do yard work.
- Plan an energy renewal at least once a week in the form of a yoga or Tai Chi lesson.
- Learn to say "no" and mean it.
- Lay out things (clothes, books) you'll need the night before. This is especially helpful for children of all ages.
- Learn to do nothing as a way of calming your mind and body.
- Train children and friends to respect your quiet time and thank them often for that.
- Arrange for your bank to do as much of your banking as possible by mail and phone (e.g., ordering new checks by phone; automatic processing of savings deductions from paychecks).
- Have an automatic reply for door-to-door salespeople and telephone solicitors. Some people let the answering machine screen their phone calls.
- Ask friends to help you find a job, service or product; establish an information network.
- Get rid of your television set.
- Take time to eat and sleep properly.
- Keep a shopping list on your bulletin board so that you can jot down needs as they develop.
- Obtain all major department store catalogs, compare prices, and shop by telephone.
- Make a list of errands which can be done in the same shopping center or area of town so that you save time and gas by a one-trip consolidation.

- Plan all doctor appointments for the same day (e.g., gynecologist, eye doctor, dentist).
- Read the food specials so you can stock up on staples by the case.
- Purchase and use a grocery item adder or mini-calculator for shopping to assess the total before reaching the check-out counter.
- Use waiting time at the laundry or auto repair shop to go to the library, shop, read or write letters.
- Buy two books of stamps at a time to avoid continually running out.
- Refuse to buy cars, furniture or other items needing babying or special care.
- Buy simple, easy-to-maintain clothing which can be laundered. Give up ironing.

At Work. . .

- Place a large planning calendar on the wall so you are aware of key meetings and deadlines.
- Carry a small appointment calendar to record appointments as they are made.
- Keep a small notebook or index cards with you for writing down ideas as they occur.
- Plan time several months in advance for ongoing priority projects.
- Give yourself deadlines for assignments and tasks.
- Schedule breakfast and lunch meetings instead of evening meetings.
- When holding meetings, allow participants to come and go as their contribution is needed and completed. It is not always necessary for everyone to stay at the meeting for the entire time.
- Open your mail in the latter part of the morning or in the afternoon instead of at 9:00 a.m. There is always a variety of items in the mail, and these varied items distract your thoughts away from your top priority items.
- Pull files or other materials before you leave the office.
- Maintain an "interruption log" for analysis.
- Limit your attendance at meetings.
- Go through your past correspondence and find your best paragraphs on every common subject that normally occurs in your writing. Compile them all into a loose-leaf binder or in the

computer, organized by subject and number each paragraph. To create new correspondence, just leaf through your book until you find the paragraph you want to use. Use the code numbers in the order you want them entered.

- Use written communication, telephone conference calls or e-mail in place of meetings.
- Delegate your attendance at meetings to subordinates.
- Hold stand-up meetings if possible.
- Set target dates for completion of every project.
- Save all the paper trivia for a three-hour session once a month.
- Clear your desk of all projects except the one at hand.
- Learn to develop an intense concentration span for everything you do.
- Send short messages by post card or e-mail instead of writing letters or making phone calls.
- Make a list of things which can be done in five minutes or less. Whenever you have a few minutes and don't know what to do, go over your short-task list.
- Designate a place for everything and keep it there.
- Set priorities for your first concerns each morning and attend to them one by one.
- Don't schedule meetings for the sake of meetings.
- Prepare meeting agendas and stick to them.
- Concentrate on only one thing at time to avoid fragmentation.
- Stop shuffling through papers, avoiding decisions; handle each paper only once.
- Ask yourself: "How could I best spend this moment?"
- Don't waste the time of other people or intrude on their quiet periods.
- Avoid negative people who sap you of energy and who have a "can't do" approach to the world and their work.
- Stay in touch with enthusiastic people who motivate you by their productivity and zest for life.
- Know when you have reached your peak of efficiency and stop when you feel tired.
- Spend less time on the phone.
- Train yourself to cut down on coffee breaks, trivial conversation, and other time wasters during office hours.
- Eat a simple, sustaining lunch to prevent afternoon grogginess.

- Respond to letters on the original letter; photocopy and file it. Or fax the response and no photocopy is necessary.
- List tomorrow's priorities before leaving the office today.
- If someone asks, "Have a minute?" say "no" if you don't.
- Arrange your office with your back to the door.
- If you can, have all calls screened. List who should be put through.
- Set time limits for meetings.

Travel...

- Keep a list of items to pack taped inside your suitcase lid for hasty departures.
- If you are frequently away overnight, keep a tote bag packed with the items you'll need: deodorant, soap, toothbrush and paste, curlers, makeup, razor, nail polish and remover, extra traveler's checks, coins for stamps, soft drinks, tips or parking.
- Use airport waiting time to read, write letters, or work on your laptop.
- Utilize long commuting trips for dictating correspondence, studying language by cassette or listening to books on tape.
- Carry a crushable, all-purpose suitcase aboard the airplane to avoid checking and awaiting baggage.

Relationships...

- Assess how much time a new relationship will require before leaping into it.
- Deal with resentments or bad feelings as soon as you recognize them to preclude hours of wasted time fretting.
- Spend more time with people who really matter to you.

22

Stress Relief: Avoiding Burnout

Mention the word "burnout" and almost everyone within earshot will quickly admit — almost proudly — that they are experiencing it. Images abound: dying embers, smoldering wicks, and cold, gray ashes...

What does burnout have to do with stress? What are the causes and symptoms? Is it treatable?

Burnout and Stress

Burnout is linked to distress. Remember that stress is neutral; it only becomes "good" or "bad" from your reactions to it. Coping well results in eustress, which can be a motivator and energizer. Ineffective coping results in distress, which will eventually lead to physical and psychological problems. When distress is left untreated, burnout gradually sets in.

The People-Work Connection

Who is at risk of burning out? What happens on the job to lead to burnout? Everyone is susceptible, especially when a working environment deteriorates.

It is not the job itself which causes burnout; it is your personal negative reaction. Even exciting and fun jobs can lead to disaster if you begin to care less and less about work and begin to seek more and more of your enjoyment and fulfillment from sources outside the job.

When you begin a new job, you are usually enthused, fired up, dedicated, full of energy, excited, willing to work hard. When this kind of good "fit" exists between you and your work, enthusiasm, satisfaction, productivity, achievement, and personal growth usually result. But when a poor fit either exists or develops over time, the job becomes less rewarding.

In time, job stagnation turns into frustration; major disappointments, unresolved problems, and irritations lead to impatience and intolerance. You may begin to question your effectiveness on the job — even the value of the job itself. Eventually, if no intervention occurs, you will probably become more and more apathetic. You punch in; you punch out, doing the bare minimum required to get by.

This is burnout; a total physical and emotional exhaustion combined with a sense of frustration, powerlessness, and apathy — all resulting from job distress.

Warning Signals

It doesn't happen in a flash, with lots of sparks and smoke. Usually, there are several telltale warning signals that something is smoldering. First, comes a gradual, progressive increase in emotional and physical exhaustion. The rest and replenishment so badly needed never come. Second, burnout is usually associated with *job* distress. Your reactions to the normal stresses of work can lead to stagnation, frustration, powerlessness, and apathy.

Everybody who works is susceptible. (A word of caution to homemakers and students: even though your work is nontraditional, you are just as much at risk as those in other occupations.) Finally, the distress on the job spills over into the other areas of your life, resulting in burnout.

Your response to conditions at work (including organizational, environmental, and people stressors), despite its impact on your personal life, is not the whole story. You bring stressors to the job (people, work, money, leisure, mind, and body) which affect the work atmosphere. Your reaction to both sets of stressors, those from the job and those you bring to the job, interact to fuel the burnout process.

Since you and your job both contribute to burnout, you and your employer have a joint opportunity and responsibility to recognize the symptoms and deal with the issues before they become too serious. Employers and workers must point to themselves, not to each other, for causing the problem. At the same time, each must seek coping strategies and buffers which will prevent burnout before it starts, or relieve it if it exists.

Burnout is not terminal, usually. It is infectious, however, and can spread like wildfire through your personal and professional life if ignored. While everyone becomes singed around the edges at times from pushing too hard or ignoring the warning signs, burnout is treatable.

What is even more encouraging is that burnout is not inevitable. It can be prevented.

Burning Issues

You spent some important time in Chapters 4-9 finding out the specific stressors which created distress in your personal life. If left untreated these stressors can spill over into your job and increase your chances of burning out. Your job can also contribute unique factors which may lead from distress to burnout. Use the following list of potential work stressors as a checklist to assess your job situation. The more issues which exist, the more likely burnout could begin.

Organization
- Unclear or too many rules, regulations, or policies
- Poor management
- No career ladder available
- Frequent changes within the workplace without input from the people affected
- Unclear, changing, or lack of job descriptions
- Decisions constantly made by supervisors without input from employees
- Few external awards for a job well done
- Work overload, underload
- Overpromotion, underpromotion
- Absence of programs for employee renewal, training, or development

People
- Lack of cooperation among employees or departments
- Poor supervision
- Complaining and backbiting by employees
- Predominantly negative feedback from supervisors
- Lack of informal or formal staff meetings
- Lack of recognition by supervisors for good work
- Little or no faith, trust, or openness among staff members

Environment
- Poor communication within the workplace
- No freedom for creativity, mistakes, or differences of opinion
- Problems remain unsolved for long periods of time
- Employee stagnation (same office and/or responsibilities year after year)
- Office politics
- Distressful working conditions (lack, of privacy, loud noises)
- Responsibility but no authority to carry out decisions

People Symptoms
A fever is a symptom of an infection in the body. Burnout also has some unique symptoms which can act as a warning if you know what to look for. The five sets of symptoms presented below begin with *physical*

reactions and progress through the *spiritual*. Symptoms in all five areas seem to develop sequentially, but become progressively worse when all are present in your life.

How long does it take for someone to burn out? It can take a few months or a few decades. Many people never experience burnout. *You are more at risk any time you give in to the frustrations and give up trying to cope.*

The symptoms presented here are rarely all present in one person. Look for those which are most characteristic of your coping style. Look for symptoms in your coworkers. Be especially alert to the *physical* and *social* symptoms, because burnout is most easily treated in these stages. Yet the tendency is to ignore these symptoms. No one can ignore the psychological and spiritual symptoms that occur later, as they destroy the individual and threaten the workplace. Everyone wants to help then, but by that time the victim may be very resistant, denying that a problem even exists. Early detection and prevention are the keys.

Physical Symptoms (your body will be the first to go)
- extended fatigue and persistent tension
- feeling drained or used up
- difficulty sleeping, falling asleep, or feeling rested
- suffering from a generally poor physical condition
- maintaining poor eating habits and exhibiting weight changes
- increased potential for digestive disorders, lower back pains, and coronary problems.

Social Symptoms (after your body goes, friends are not far behind)
- decreased importance of relationships
- increased irritability (you become a real grouch)
- having difficulty dealing with people; less patience, more resentment and anger, more tendency to lash out
- more complaints about work
- less time spent in pleasant conversations with family or friends
- putting off personal interactions both at work and at home
- a gradual preference for isolation
- reluctance to share feelings with spouse, friends, colleagues
- increased clock-watching
- diminished sense of humor

Psychological Symptoms (now that your body and friends are gone, your mind is next)
- feelings of being overloaded with information and details
- beginning to avoid tasks that involve thinking
- finding it difficult, if not impossible, to concentrate
- problems on the job become more and more difficult to handle
- demonstrating inaccurate, poor judgment
- increased aggression and cynicism toward people
- curt and sarcastic responses to people
- setting unrealistic goals
- finding it difficult to go to work each day
- a tendency to stereotype colleagues and customers at work
- increasingly "going by the book"
- feelings of alienation from people and tasks
- deepening feelings of boredom
- missing deadlines with little or no remorse
- feeling as if you're always meeting *someone else's* needs
- increasing levels of unexpressed anger and frustration
- increased suspicion, distrust, resentment
- feelings of helplessness and hopelessness
- mood swings
- overwhelming feelings of depression, pessimism, and failure
- use of drugs and alcohol as solutions

Spiritual Symptoms (when everything else is gone, . . .)
- seriously doubting one's own personal values and beliefs
- feeling threatened by others
- questioning your contributions to society, family, work
- impulsive and major changes in lifestyle (divorce, running away, quitting the job)
- experiencing feelings of emptiness, anxiety, disillusionment
- constantly looking for the easy solution or magic answer
- denying that a problem exists or blaming others for the problem
- rejecting all offers for help
- possible suicide attempts

Work Symptoms

When something goes wrong in the workplace, the word spreads and the organization, no matter how large or small, suffers and is weakened. One or two people may be in the process of burning out and the ripples will spread. Those who are burning out will be given more slack. Their symptoms will be ignored. Work begins to pile up, and staff members who are not victims become overloaded with the undone work. Overloaded co-workers may express anger toward the burnout victims.

You can see what begins to happen. Eventually, the whole workplace can begin to burn out if no prevention or intervention takes place. It is very important to be able to recognize the symptoms in yourself, your colleagues, and your workplace, so you can do something about it.

Here are some typical symptoms of *organizational burnout:*

- a pattern of absenteeism evolves (i.e., increased use of sick days, extended lunches and breaks)
- high staff turnover rate
- complaints surface about performance — from colleagues, management, and the public
- lower motivation, lack of initiative
- higher frustration levels
- scapegoating organizational leaders
- depersonalized services and interactions
- avoidance of certain tasks or people
- declines in productivity, quality of work, service
- interdepartmental competition and friction
- rigid boundaries evolve between offices and departments
- staff roles and functions become fixed
- deadlines are missed
- declining level of efficiency, diminished interest in work
- persistent failure to perform required tasks
- increased conflicts with authority
- arbitrary decision-making
- acting-out behavior emerges (e.g., silent withdrawal, destructive criticism, raising irrelevant issues)
- unwillingness to engage in conflict-resolution or problem-solving
- backbiting, nitpicking, sabotage
- use of alcohol or other drugs on the job
- psychosomatic illnesses emerge (e.g., hypertension, ulcers, colitis, strokes, migraines, tension headaches)

Burnout Buffers

Hang in there! Burnout is treatable. The solutions lie in whatever will rekindle the flame for you. Remember, burnout symptoms are unique to each victim. Your burnout buffers must also reflect this individuality.

Your first step in learning to spark again is knowing and recognizing your own symptoms. After you have completed an analysis of your situation, do not wait to get started. Remember, the longer you allow yourself to suffer with burnout symptoms, the more difficult it will be to light your fire! Prevention is a key concept for coping with burnout, not only in yourself but also in the workplace. The buffers listed below are proven, effective techniques for organizations. Look them over carefully and, if necessary, modify them to fit your situation.

The dozens of buffers you reviewed in Chapters 12-17 are excellent resources for coping with burnout on a personal level, especially the Work Buffers. In addition, you may want to consider:

- accentuating the positive in your job (concentrating on accomplishment, conversing, sharing jokes, making positive feedback a personal commitment)
- developing transition time activities to decompress (see Chapter 21)
- personalizing your work environment with photos, paintings, flowers, sculptures, special calendars
- becoming involved in meaningful projects or committees which can bring variety to work
- evaluating the meaningfulness of your work tasks so you can determine where your personal investment of time and energy should be directed.

The organization, through its managers and supervisors, has some options which can relieve burnout symptoms. The symptoms must not be ignored because the more people feel burned out, the closer the entire organization comes to snuffing the collective flames of productivity and job satisfaction. If you are in a position of power or influence, we urge you to consider:

- supporting innovation and creativity
- improving feedback to employees
- increasing employee participation in decisions that directly affect them
- when no compromise is feasible, clearly explaining why

- giving information to supervisors and other employees as problems arise
- developing realistic, complete job descriptions
- developing clearer, more positively stated policies and procedures
- establishing flexible leaves and support services
- improving training programs
- creating better division of labor
- changing standard operating procedures
- redesigning jobs
- rotating jobs
- designing and encouraging lateral job transfers
- encouraging team efforts with goal-setting, problem-solving
- suggesting and supporting cross-training
- modifying contacts with the public to reduce distress
- creating mentorships so that newly hired employees have a clear orientation to the workplace, including job stressors
- limiting job spillover by discouraging overtime and encouraging breaks, lunch hours, and vacation time
- suggesting professional help (medical, psychological)
- modifying reward systems based on employee needs, desires
- changing management style, organizational structure
- offering stress management and time management training (the authors — and hundreds of other qualified consultants — are available!)
- providing career counseling
- limiting length of meetings
- creating evaluation procedures that provide positive feedback and opportunities for growth
- supporting creation of positive work environments
- celebrating personal and departmental successes, milestones, events
- building-in recreation and play time
- encouraging and rewarding individual efforts at physical fitness and wellness

Burnout Bibliography

Cherniss, *Professional Burnout in Human Service Organizations*
Freudenberger, *Burn-Out: The High Cost of High Achievement*
Freudenberger, *Women's Burnout*
Pines, *Burnout: From Tedium to Personal Growth*
Veninga, *The Work-Stress Connection: How to Cope With Job Burnout*
Welch, *Beyond Burnout*

For a more complete description of these books, please see
"Suggested Readings," page 179.

23

Last Words

$\mathcal{Y}$es, it's the end of this book. But, it is only the beginning of your exciting discoveries in stress relief.

Our desire is that you would feel a sense of hope and a sense of accomplishment for taking the first steps. You've recognized that you are an "owner" of stress. Now you have a "do-it-yourself maintenance manual," and you know how to use it to work on your stress — to improve, to grow, to find more meaning, and to become healthier and more satisfied with yourself.

As you continue to take more responsibility for your life and the path it takes, we offer the following summary thoughts:

• *Stop stress before it starts:* Be proactive and preventative by using techniques and actions to deal with whatever is happening in your life as it is happening.

• *Watch how you talk to yourself:* Your mind and what you allow it to tell you will determine the quality and the length of your life.

• *Know yourself:* Recognize your unique physical and psychological symptoms of distress and use these personal warnings to adjust your attitude and take action.

• *Let it go:* Be brutally honest with yourself. If you are using stress as a crutch, an attention-getter, or as an excuse... recognize what you are doing and get off of it.

• *Be patient:* Chances are your stress has been building for months or even years. Accept the possibility that it may take a period of time to modify your lifestyle and find what you are seeking. Stop driving yourself and be more loving and patient with yourself.

• *Depend on others:* You may not think you are the most likable person when you are reacting to life's stressors, but encourage yourself to accept the fact that you are lovable. Add people into your life because support from others is such an important way to reach your goals and to find meaning, health and balance. Allow yourself to be supported. Ask for support.

• *Develop a shopping list:* What will work for you in your search for more meaning, balance and health will depend on the attitudes and the actions you identify and make your own. Having lots of possibilities from which to choose will make success a definite reality.

• *Be honest and realistic:* No one is perfect, and even the most highly motivated people will slip occasionally. When that happens, have a supportive talk with yourself. Acknowledge the truth about who you are and what you are doing to live the life you want.

• *Stress management is forever:* You'll always own some amount of stress. Stress management is simply living a healthy, balanced, meaningful life. It's a lifelong process of discovery and challenge. Embark willingly.

• *Have fun:* Talk to yourself about how you are worth the effort to change; grow; be healthier, and find more meaning. Life is not worth dying for because you pushed too hard. Ease up, enjoy and have fun...today and every day!

Suggested Readings

Ackerman, *Getting Rich*. NY: A & W Publishers, Inc. 1981.
Great book for women who are typically intimidated by financial matters and who want an introduction to money management with women's needs in mind.

Alberti, *Making Yourself Heard: A Guide to Assertive Relationships*. NY: Guilford Publications, 1986.
On audiotape, the comprehensive self-guided assertiveness training program emphasizes relationships, not "me first" attitudes. Whether your goal is to gain elementary assertive skills, to approach life with more confidence, or to develop your abilities to deal with family, close friends, or difficult circumstances, this six-session audio cassette program can provide deep and lasting results.

Alberti and Emmons, *Your Perfect Right: A Guide To Assertive Living* (Seventh Edition). San Luis Obispo, CA: Impact Publishers, Inc., 1995.
The first book designed for the layperson interested in developing more assertive behavior. Contains a supplementary section on technical materials for the professional.

Albrecht, *Stress and the Manager: Making It Work for You*. Englewood Cliffs, NJ: Prentice-Hall, Inc., 1979.
This book contains a well-presented description of the stress concept. The author presents an analysis of "wellness" which is a good stimulus to learn more about holistic approaches to health.

Ardell, *High Level Wellness: An Alternative to Doctors, Drugs, and Disease*. Emmaus, PA: Rodale Press, 1977.
A guidebook to optimal well-being that tells you the things you need to know to shape a richly positive lifestyle that will keep you younger longer. The book includes self-tests you can use to determine your present level of wellness; ways to integrate the five dimensions vital to your health needs; strategies for shaping your personal environment to reduce fatigue and lower stress.

Beckfield, *Master Your Panic...and Take Back Your Life!: Twelve Treatment Sessions to Overcome High Anxiety*. San Luis Obispo, CA: Impact Publishers, Inc., 1994.
Twenty-four million adult Americans suffer from some form of anxiety disorder, and tens of thousands seek professional help each year. This practical, self-empowering book parallels an actual treatment program for overcoming debilitating panic attacks. Readers are guided, step-by-step, through twelve self-help "treatment sessions." Proven, research-based methods are presented in easy-to-follow instructions, accompanied by numerous case examples.

Benson, *The Relaxation Response.* NY: Avon Books, 1976.
Synthesis of modern discoveries and religious/philosophic literature regarding the effects of meditation techniques. Benson describes how to deal constructively with the pressures of contemporary society through a meditation technique he calls the "relaxation response."

Bible.
Choose from a wide range of excellent versions. But most importantly, set aside a short (or long) period of time daily to allow its wisdom and richness to fill you. Caution: excess reading may lead to a deeper sense of fulfillment and meaning in your life!

Bolles, *What Color Is Your Parachute?* Berkeley, CA: Ten Speed Press, 1996 (updated annually).
Job-hunters and career-changers will appreciate this very practical manual. It tells you in step-by-step detail how to identify what you want to do with your life, how to locate the job you want, and how to convince the employer you're the best person for the job. Includes the "Quick Job-Hunting Map" which is a very useful and necessary tool in helping you eventually decide what you want to do with your life.

Bricklin, Golin and Grandinetti, *Positive Living and Health: The Complete Guide to Brain/Body Healing and Mental Empowerment.* Emmaus, PA: Rodale Press, 1990.
Over 500 pages of easy-to-read and convincing research and tips are combined to help any reader become more of a believer in the power of your mind and the power of positive thinking and living.

Briles, *The Woman's Guide to Financial Savvy.* NY: St. Martin's Press, 1981.
The author uses a down-to-earth approach to show women how to create a financial strategy. Included is a dictionary of terms that takes the mystery out of financial terminology.

Brody, *Jane Brody's Nutrition Book.* NY: W.W. Norton & Co., 1981.
This is probably the soundest and most comprehensive guide to nutrition yet available for the layperson. The twenty-seven chapters cover in detail, yet in understandable language, every aspect of nutrition from the basics of essential nutrition to reading food labels. This book is more than facts; it is a way of increasing nutritional awareness. A real pleasure to read and use.

Brown, *Stress and the Art of Biofeedback.* NY: Bantam Books, 1977.
The author provides a comprehensive explanation of how the technique of biofeedback has been used to successfully treat more than fifty major stress-related disorders.

Campbell, *Beyond the Power Struggle: Dealing with Conflict in Love and Work.* San Luis Obispo, CA: Impact Publishers, Inc., 1984.
In this book, the author-psychologist shows how *both-and* relationships value *both* individuals *and* avoid the conflict that often results from an either-or approach. The author gives hope: "Differences are inevitable, but conflict and struggle are not."

Charland, *Career Shifting: Starting Over in a Changing Economy.* Holbrook, MA: Bob
    Adams, Inc., 1993.
An invaluable one-volume career survival kit for changing times. It will help you
understand how skills and occupations are evolving today — and learn how to take
more control over your career by updating your skills.

Cherniss, *Professional Burnout in Human Service Organizations.* NY: Praeger, 1980.
The author of this book paints a picture of what happens to a person when he or she
becomes the so-called "professional" in the helping professions.

Chopra, *Ageless Body, Timeless Mind: The Quantum Alternative to Growing Old.* NY:
    Harmony Books, 1993.
Contrary to your traditional notions of aging, you can learn to direct the way your
body metabolizes time. This book combines mind-body medicine with current
antiaging research to show why and how the effects of aging are largely preventable.
By intervening at the level where belief becomes biology, we can achieve our
unbounded potential.

Combs, *Hearing Loss Help.* San Luis Obispo, CA: Impact Publishers, Inc., 1992.
This popular self-help guide for hearing impaired persons and their friends and
families is filled with practical information on how to improve everyday
communication, create better listening conditions, understand the physical and
psychological effects of hearing loss, choose among the many varieties of hearing
assistance devices, get good professional care, and more.

Comfort, *The Joy of Sex.* NY: Simon and Schuster, Inc., 1986.
Very popular book discussing the central importance of unanxious, responsible, and
happy sexuality in the lives of normal people.

Cousins, *Head First: The Biology of Hope.* NY: E.P. Dutton, 1989.
In his book, *Anatomy of an Illness,* the author describes his recovery from a terminal
illness through traditional medical treatment and non-traditional approaches. In this
book, he explains the mind-body connections, in the form of hope, that create the
impossible in people.

Cousins, *The Healing Heart: Antidotes to Panic and Helplessness.* NY: W.W. Norton
    and Company, Inc., 1983.
The author deals with an illness that is the most common cause of death in the U.S.:
the heart attack. He tells of his own massive heart attack and the importance of the
patient's essential role in combating serious illness. It is also a story of a team effort, a
partnership, between the patient and his physician.

Covey, *First Things First: To Live, To Learn, To Leave a Legacy.* NY: Simon and
    Schuster, Inc., 1994.
Helps you understand why your first things aren't first. The book transcends the
traditional time management prescriptions of faster, harder, smarter, and more.
Rather than offering another clock, it provides you with a compass because where
you're headed is more important than how fast you're going.

Covey, *The 7 Habits of Highly Effective People*. NY: Simon and Schuster, Inc., 1989.
The author presents a holistic, integrated, principle-centered approach for solving
personal land professional problems. He reveals a step-by-step pathway for living with
fairness, integrity, honesty, and human dignity — principles that give us the security
to adapt to change, and the wisdom and power to take advantage of the opportunities
that change creates.

Dinkmeyer and McKay, *Raising a Responsible Child*. NY: Simon and Schuster, Inc.,
 1973.
Offers specific family-centered, egalitarian methods that benefit parents as well as
children. Helps create a healthy environment for child growth.

Dossey, *Healing Words: The Power of Prayer and The Practice of Medicine*. NY:
 HarperCollins Publishers, 1993.
In this book the author shares the latest evidence linking prayer, healing, and medicine
and calls for a new integration of science and spirituality.

Downing, *The Massage Book,* Westminster, MD: Bookworks, 1972.
This books tells you why massage is important and then tells you how to massage each
and every part of the body. The drawings are clear and the instructions simple, easy to
follow and fun!

Dreikurs, Gould, and Corsini, *Family Council,* Chicago: Contemporary Books, Inc.,
 1974.
The Dreikurs Technique is a way of "putting an end to war" between parents and
children (and between children and children). This book is based on the idea that not
only are people equal, but that they should be treated as equal. The key is the family
council, a problem-solving and communication-building technique. The authors
explain, step-by-step and point-by-point, how to introduce the concept into a home.

Emmons and Alberti, *Accepting Each Other: Individuality and Intimacy in Your Loving
 Relationship*. San Luis Obispo, CA: Impact Publishers, Inc., 1991.
Contrary to popular (and some professional) notions, intimacy is not just sex, not just
unlimited openness. In this book, the authors offer the most comprehensive view yet
of intimate relationships. Built around the theme of *acceptance*, the book describes the
interaction of six key dimensions of intimacy: the *attraction* which brings partners
together, the quality of their *communications*, their ongoing *commitment* to staying
together, the *enjoyment* each derives from the partnership, their individual and mutual
life *purpose*, the degree of *trust* which exists in the relationship.

Fanning, *Get It All Done and Still Be Human*. Radnor, PA: Chilton Book Co., 1979.
A quick-reading, handy guide to help you learn to get the most out of your day. There
are separate chapters on time-gobblers and how to starve them, time stretchers, and
human tools for managing your time.

Fast, *The Pleasure Book*. NY: Stein & Day Publishers, 1975.
This is a browsing book. Its goal is to teach you how to pursue new pleasures in life
by providing one- or two-page explanations of different experiences. The simple
pleasures of the wind in your face, day dreaming, white water inner tubing, long
baths, perfume and over 60 other potential "peak experiences" come alive on the page,
rekindling pleasant memories or creating the desire to try something new. It really is a
pleasure book!

Fisher, *Rebuilding: When Your Relationship Ends* (Second Edition). San Luis Obispo, CA: Impact Publishers, Inc., 1992.
Provides building blocks for a nineteen-step process for putting your life back together after a divorce. Includes a useful Divorce Adjustment Scale and relationship material on many topics including, in the newest edition, adaptation, fear, openness, relatedness and purpose. Also available on audiotape.

Foster, *Prayer: Finding the Heart's True Home*. NY: HarperCollins Publishers, 1992.
The author offers a warm, compelling, and sensitive primer on prayer, helping you to understand, experience, and practice it in its many forms. He clarifies the prayer process, answers common misconceptions, and shows the way into prayers of contemplation, healing, blessing, forgiveness, and rest.

Frankl, *Man's Search for Meaning*. NY: Washington Square Press, Inc., 1967.
One man's experiences in the concentration camps of Nazi Germany. The author explains how he could find life worth living with every possession lost, all key relationships severed, suffering from hunger, cold and brutality, expecting extermination hourly. His message is an important one for you if you are searching for more meaning and fulfillment in your life.

Freudenberger, *Burnout: The High Cost of High Achievement*. NY: Anchor Press, 1980.
This book is designed for the overachiever who wants to deal with the symptoms of burnout before he/she is overcome. The author gives the reader suggestions on how to put the vitality back into one's life with workable cures.

Freudenberger and North, *Women's Burnout*. NY: Doubleday, 1985.
The authors believe that one of the most pressing issues facing women today is burnout. They examine the specifics for women and how women might begin to reverse the effects.

Gaedwag, (Ed.), *Inner Balance: The Power of Holistic Healing*. Englewood cliffs, NJ: Prentice-Hall, Inc., 1979.
This book highlights, through chapters written by thoughtful professionals in the health care system, that a better approach to healing can be achieved through methods of controlling the stress response. The editor's aim was to synthesize three aspects of humans — body, mind, and spirit — specifically related to health and disease.

Gendlin, *Focusing*. NY: Bantam Books, 1981.
The author provides the philosophical background and then the specific instructions to this technique of self-therapy that teaches you to identify and change the way your personal problems concretely exist in your body. The book guides you to the deepest level of awareness within your body where unresolved problems exist. The steps consist of felt change: when each step is done correctly, there is physical relief, a profound release of tension.

Gibran, *The Prophet*. NY: Alfred Knopf, Inc., 1965.
The insight of this author from Lebanon has continued to capture the hearts of humans. Gibran speaks poetically, yet so incisively and understandably about everyday life: love, giving, feedom, pain, talking, time, joy, self-knowledge, and other important topics. His words touch the heart and leave a lasting impression.

Goldberg and Kaufman, *Natural Sleep: How to Get Your Share*. Emmaus, PA: Rodale
    Press, Inc., 1979.
This is a fun-to-read, meticulously researched book on sleep with effective procedures
for achieving sleep without pills. Includes bedtime rituals, massage, breathing and
relaxing techniques, hypnosis, herbal remedies, and more.

Hastings, Fadiman and Gordon (eds.), *Health for the Whole Person: The Complete
    Guide to Holistic Medicine*. NY: Bantam Books, 1980.
If you want a comprehensive source book on holistic approaches to health, this is it.
The extensive, annotated bibliography can direct you to the best additional
information on such topics as biofeedback, Chinese medicine and acupuncture, natural
childbirth, chiropractic, herbal medicines, psychic healing, and nutrition therapy. A
very complete review of alternate health techniques.

Heath, *Long Distance Caregiving: A Survival Guide for Far Away Caregivers*. San Luis
    Obispo, CA: Impact Publishers, Inc., 1993.
Tells you everything you need to know to survive the challenge of caring for your
distant relative. In a succinct, no-nonsense manner it describes: how to quickly find
people in your older relative's town to help with day-to-day needs, how to prepare for
scheduled and unscheduled visits, how to handle emergencies, how to organize and
carry off the all-important family meetings, and much, much more.

Kubler-Ross, *Death: The Final Stage of Growth*. Englewood Cliffs, NJ: Prentice-Hall,
    Inc., 1975.
From her own personal views and experiences and from comparisons with how
various cultures view death and dying, Kubler-Ross answers such questions as: Why
do we treat death as a taboo? What are the sources of our fears? How do we express
our grief and accept the death of a person close to us? How can we prepare for our
own death? She shows how, through an acceptance of our finiteness, we can grow, for
death provides a key to the meaning of human existence.

Kubler-Ross, *On Death and Dying*. NY: Macmillan Publishing Co., Inc., 1964.
Dr. Ross attempts to focus on the dying patient so that we call all learn from that
patient the anxieties, fears and hopes in dying.

Kushner, *When Bad Things Happen to Good People*. NY: Avon Books, 1981.
This is not an abstract book about God and theology. It is a very personal book about
the author's rethinking of everything he had been taught about God and God's way
after the tragic death of his son. It provides great insight, comfort and strength and
helps you understand that God can fill the deepest needs of an anguished heart.

Kuzma, *Prime-Time Parenting*. NY: Rawson, Wade Publishers, Inc., 1980.
An innovative, comprehensive program for busy parents. It offers a unique perspective
on parenting, plus hundreds of practical suggestions and exercises. Chapter 9,
"Shortcuts to Prime Time Parenting," is especially creative and helpful.

Lakein, *How to Get Control of Your Time and Your Life*. NY: New American Library,
    1974.
An excellent guide to managing personal and professional time. The author explains
how to set short and long-term goals, establish priorities, organize a daily schedule
and achieve better self-understanding. Tips are included on building willpower,
creating quiet time, defeating unpleasant tasks, and keeping yourself on target.

Lazarus, Lazarus, and Fay, *Don't Believe it for a Minute!: Forty Toxic Ideas that are Driving You Crazy.* San Luis Obispo, CA: Impact Publishers, Inc., 1993.
Two psychologists and a psychiatrist debunk forty common misbeliefs that can lead to depression, anxiety and guilt. The authors tell you how to fix these misbeliefs by giving the "antidote" to each toxic idea. This book is great for individuals who are confused, anxious; couples wishing to explore their beliefs about each other and about their relationship; patients in therapy; family members and friends of patients; those who counsel or work with individuals who harbor toxic ideas.

LeShan, *How to Meditate: A Guide to Self-Discovery.* Boston: Little, Brown & Co., 1974.
This book has a simple, straightforward approach that demystifies meditation. The content covers psychological effects, basic types, structured and unstructured, as well as choosing your own meditation path.

McKay and Dinkmeyer, *How You Feel is Up to You: The Power of Emotional Choice.* San Luis Obispo, CA: Impact Publishers, Inc., 1994.
Turn your feelings from liabilities ("I'm a victim") to assets ("I can manage"). You can decide how you want to feel. Here's a practical self-improvement tool kit to help handle guilt, anger, depression, stress, and anxiety. Provides useful information and straightforward procedures to help you enhance your awareness of feelings — and learn how to manage strong negative emotions and increase joy and happiness.

Millman, *Secret of the Peaceful Warrior: A Story About Courage and Love.* Tiburon, CA: H. J. Kramer, Inc., 1991.
What looks like a children's book also has a strong message to all adults about overcoming fears and changing the world through courage and love. The other books by the author are just as powerful: *Way of a Peaceful Warrior* and *The Warrior Athlete.*

Moe, *Make Your Paycheck Last.* Hawthorne, NJ: The Career Press, 1993.
The author explains that it is not so much how much you make but what you decide to do with it. It is a self-help workbook approach that starts with setting goals, laying out a plan and living by it. Easy to read and apply.

Moyers, *Healing and the Mind.* NY: Doubleday, 1993.
Either read this book or watch the PBS video series if you are interested in the two questions that shaped this book/video: How do thoughts and feelings influence health? and How is healing related to the mind? The search reaches into history, geography, cultures, and practices for the answers.

Munsch, *Love You Forever.* Ontario, Canada: Firefly Books Ltd., 1986.
A tear-jerker of a child's book also for adults of all ages. It is the simple story of a little boy going to be a man and the story of the enduring nature of parents' love and how it crosses generations. Read it to your children. Read it to yourself!! OFTEN!

Novak, *The World's Wisdom: Sacred Texts of the World's Religions.* NY: HarperCollins Publishers, 1994.
This book is an essential collection of the world's most profound and enlightening wisdom, a world Bible for our time, containing sacred readings from Buddhist, Hindu, Confucian, Taoist, Jewish, Christian, Islamic, and primal religion sources. Selections were chosen for their inspirational power and instructional value.

Peale, *The Power of Positive Thinking*. NY: Prentice-Hall, Inc., 1956.
This is a classic that remains popular for only one reason— the ideas work! Dr. Peale demonstrates the power of faith in action. A proper attitude can change lives and win success in all things. This book outlines the steps to achieve any goal.

Peck, *The Road Less Traveled: A New Psychology of Love, Traditional Values and Spiritual Growth*. NY: Simon and Schuster, 1978.
The author, using his own psychiatric case studies, suggests ways in which confronting and resolving our problems — and suffering through the changes — can enable you to reach a higher level of self-understanding. His simple yet profoundly convincing style helps you understand the nature of loving relationships, how to recognize true compatibility, how to distinguish dependency from love, how to become one's own person, how to be a more sensitive parent.

Perkins and Rhoades, *The Women's Financial Survival Handbook*. NY: New American Libary, 1980.
The authors believe that women need to fully understand their financial situation so they can both protect and take care of themselves. They insist that women can no longer keep their heads in the sand when thinking about their financial futures.

Phelps and Austin, *The Assertive Woman: A New Look*. San Luis Obispo, CA: Impact Publishers, Inc., 1987.
A clearly written book for a systematic attack upon the self-denying lifestyle so many women have been conditioned to accept.

Pines, Aronson and Kafry. *Burnout, from Tedium to Personal Growth*. NY: The Free Press. 1981.
The authors do an excellent job of discussing the causes of burnout obtained through thousands of case studies and presentinig the strategies one might use to combat it both in and outside of the work environment.

Preston, *Growing Beyond Emotional Pain: Action Plans for Healing*. San Luis Obispo, CA: Impact Publishers, Inc., 1993.
This book will help you become one of those who knows what works, and what does not, in handling the emotional blows of life by offering proven, psychologically sound procedures. The author's nine "action plans for healing" — each one specific, practical and effective — are firmly grounded in solid psychological research.

Preston, *You Can Beat Depression: A Guide to Prevention and Recovery* (Second Edition). San Luis Obispo, CA: Impact Publishers, Inc., 1996
Depressed individuals, even those in treatment, can benefit from these self-help approaches. As an adjunct to therapy or medication, as a self-help guide, and as a source of understanding, this is an insightful, practical book.

Robbins, *Unlimited Power*. NY: Ballantine Books, 1986.
This book is about power over yourself, not power over other people. The author provides convincing evidence and practical techniques to harness your mind to create what you want. He shows you that your state of mind determines what you can and can't do, and that all successful results can be modeled and duplicated. Captivating reading.

Ryan and Travis, *Wellness Workbook*. Berkeley, CA: Ten Speed Press, 1981.
Once you have completed our book, the *Wellness Workbook* is highly recommended as a follow up. It will teach you how to transcend and go beyond the basics in breathing, communicating, eating, playing, finding meaning, moving, thinking, sensing, and feeling. It is really a fun workbook filled with priceless tidbits of insight and information.

Saunders and Remsberg, *The Stress-Proof Child*. NY: Holt, Rinehart and Winston, 1984.
This invaluable guide tells not only how to recognize symptoms of stress in children, but also exactly and specifically what to do about them. It explains how to teach children to deal with stress, how to value themselves, and how to become capable kids. The book explains the tested program Dr. Saunders, child psychologist, developed and implemented.

Selye, *Stress Without Distress*. NY: New American Library, 1975.
Dr. Selye synthesizes a lot of information on stress control and provides a framework for examination and refinement of your own sense of purpose. He reinforces ideas of self-responsibility and individual uniqueness in dealing with stress.

Siegel, *Love, Medicine and Miracles: Lessons Learned About Self-Healing From A Surgeon's Experience with Exceptional Patients*. NY: Harper & Row, Publishers, 1986.
This easy-to-read, yet extremely touching and powerful book is about surviving and about characteristics that survivors have in common. It is about healing, courage and love and how exceptional patients can take control in order to heal themselves.

Simonton, Matthews-Simonton and Creighton, *Getting Well Again*. NY: Bantam Books, 1980.
The authors profile the typical "cancer personality" and how positive expectations, self-awareness and self-care contribute to survival. This very readable, exciting book offers the same self-help techniques the Simontons' patients have used so successfully to reinforce usual medical treatment — techniques for learning positive attitudes, relaxation, visualization, goal setting, managing pain, exercise, and building an emotional support system. The best aspect of this book is that it is not only for cancer patients or others with serious illness but for anyone who wants to participate in maintaining his or her health.

Smith, *Caring for Your Aging Parents: A Sourcebook of Timesaving Techniques and Tips*. San Luis Obispo, CA: Impact Publishers, Inc., 1992.
A very practical how-to book for caregivers, with a step-by-step approach that divides concerns and projects into manageable, workable and, most importantly, attainable goals and tasks. Written in a very readable style, the book is chock-full of answers to problems that commonly face caregivers.

Stein, *Family Games*. NY: Macmillan Publishing Co., Inc., 1979.
With pictures and drawings, this book explains the basics of playing games anywhere as a family or with a group. Stein covers card games, tricks, picnic games, street games, party games and more.

Storr, *Solitude: A Return to the Self.* NY: Ballantine Books, 1988.
The author supports two sources of meaning and fulfillment: love and friendship as well as solitude, what goes on in the human being when he is by himself. Beautifully and insightfully written, illuminated with quotations drawn from world literature, and carefully documented with references to works of the most important psychologists, the book speaks to the profoundly neglected need of the human soul: the need to be alone.

Tyson, *Personal Finance for Dummies.* San Mateo, CA: IDG Books, 1994.
The author believes that most Americans are financially illiterate. Financial survival is not taught in schools and perhaps it should be. He connects your financial goals and problems to the rest of your life.

University of California at Berkeley, *University of California at Berkeley Wellness Letter: The Newsletter of Nutrition, Fitness, and Stress Management.*
Recently rated as the best wellness letter in print. First published in 1984, the eight-page newsletter is packed with objective facts and advice written for both the professional and the layman. About $2.00 per issue. Printed monthly. To order: University of California at Berkeley Wellness Letter, P.O. Box 420160, Palm Coast, FL 32142-9846. Highly recommended.

VanCaspel, *Money Dynamics for the 1990s.* NY: Simon and Schuster, Inc. 1988.
The author explains that the old financial rules of the '80s no longer apply and in order to make some sound money management decisions, you need to understand and apply the new rules. Topics include how to plan for your children's future college costs, information surrounding stocks, bonds and mutual finds, investment strategies for retirement and much, much more.

Veninga and Spradley, *The Work Stress Connection.* Boston: Little, Brown and Co., 1981.
The authors did in-depth interviews with people who came from a variety of walks of life, from Skid Row to Wall Street. As a result, they developed a framework to look at job burnout and related risk factors.

Walker, *Learn to Relax: 13 Ways to Reduce Tension.* Englewood Cliffs, NJ: Prentice-Hall, Inc., 1975.
Demonstrates the 13 ways to reduce tension. The author also explains helpful problem-solving and decision-making systems that can keep you from feeling overwhelmed.

Watterson, *The Authoritative Calvin and Hobbes* (one of eight books and treasuries to date of the cartoon characters, Calvin and Hobbes).
At least one of the authors, Ed, finds Calvin and Hobbes to be the key to his "humor button." Whether or not you enjoy this six-year-old comic character and stuffed tiger, you are encouraged to find some enjoyable source of laughter and perspective for your life.

Welch, Medeiros and Tate, *Beyond Burnout.* Englewood Cliffs, NJ: Prentice-Hall, 1982.
This book deals with what happens to the enthusiastic young employee who reaches the point where he/she hates to come to work. The question is what transpires, what are the symptoms and are there some particulars for some professions?

Whitsett, *Guerrilla Kindness: A Manual of Good Works, Kind Acts, and Thoughtful Deeds*. San Luis Obispo, CA: Impact Publishers, Inc., 1993.
This book is your guide. It is an action manual exploding with ideas for kindness and compassion. It is an easy-reading, open- it-anywhere collection of tactics for becoming the kinder, gentler person you'd like to be.

Whitten, *I Think My Mind is Tricking Me*. CA: Lifetimes Press, 1990.
An extremely simple yet powerful children's story, but a must for all adults, about how your minds, which are made up so much of the time, are actually tricking you. Find out how.

Williams, *Cool Cats, Calm Kids: Relaxation and Stress Management for Young People*. San Luis Obispo, CA: Impact Publishers, Inc., 1996.
A practical yet humorous stress management guide for children ages 7-12 based on nine "cat secrets" for keeping cool and calm. Includes a special section for parents, teachers, and counselors.

Young and Jones, *Sidetracked Home Executives: From Pigpen to Paradise*. NY: Time Warner Books, Inc., 1981.
The authors, sisters, were caught in the disorder of misplaced priorities, half-completed chores, and undirected energies. They analyzed their lives, set up a rotating card system that scheduled their chores on a daily, weekly, and monthly basis. They changed their attitudes, and it changed their lives. They teach their techniques with understanding, humor and patience.

Index